Have Yourself

A Very Vintage Christmas

Crafts, Decorating Tips, and Recipes, 1920s–1960s

Have Yourself

A Very Vintage Christmas

Crafts, Decorating Tips, and Recipes, 1920s–1960s

SUSAN WAGGONER

PHOTOGRAPHS BY JEFF ELKINS

Stewart, Tabori & Chang | New York

Published in 2011 by Stewart, Tabori & Chang
An imprint of ABRAMS

Text copyright © 2011 Susan Waggoner
Photographs copyright © 2011 Jeff Elkins

Waggoner, Susan.
  Have yourself a very vintage Christmas / Susan Waggoner.
    p. cm.
  ISBN 978-1-58479-923-8 (alk. paper)
  1. Christmas decorations—United States. 2. Handicraft—United States. 3.
Christmas—United States—History. I. Title.
  TT900.C4W335 2011
  745.594'12—dc22

                    2011008520

Editor: Dervla Kelly
Designer: Kay Shuckhart/Blond on Pond
Production Manager: Tina Cameron

The text of this book was composed in Adobe Caslon and Monterey.

Printed and bound in Hong Kong, China
10 9 8 7 6 5 4 3 2 1

Stewart, Tabori & Chang books are available at special discounts when purchased in quantity for pre-
miums and promotions as well as fundraising or educational use. Special editions can also be created to
specification. For details, contact specialsales@abramsbooks.com or the address below.

115 West 18th Street
New York, NY 10011
www.abramsbooks.com

Contents

Tips on Using This Book

Have Yourself a Very Vintage Christmas came about after several years of looking at old Christmas catalogues, old Christmas cards, and old family photos—my own as well as everyone else's. What I saw was a wonderful world of memory, loaded to the gills with decorations no longer made. I wanted them badly. And I didn't want the tattered, torn, and faded items that had survived in someone's attic; I wanted to see them as they might have looked when they were new. So I decided to try to make them for myself. This book is the result of those efforts, and I hope you enjoy these projects as much as I did. I also hope you'll use your creativity to make other items uniquely your own. I've included full-size card images and decorative motifs in the Art Portfolio at the back of this book. Scan or photocopy them, resize them or embellish them, and use them in your own cards, place cards, stickers, gift tags, ornaments, and accessories. I want your Christmases to be just as merry, bright, and vintage as they can be!

Tips on Using Some Basic Materials

No one involved in this book recieved any discounts, samples, or free merchandise from the manufacturers or retailers mentioned in this book. If products and retailers are listed, it's because they performed well for me and were reasonably priced. Here are some basic tips for using three products that figure in several projects in the book:

Scotch® Positionable Mounting Adhesive by 3M. I like this product for adhering paper to cardboard and other paper products for several reasons. It's dry, so it won't pucker or seep or fade ink as glue does, it doesn't require special equipment, and it's extremely easy to use—if you make a mistake positioning it, you can lift and reposition it before it bonds. It also delivers a long-lasting bond (twelve years and counting on some projects) and gives full, smooth coverage. The downside is that it can be expensive if you don't do a lot of paper crafting, since you have to buy it in paper towel–size rolls. However, if you're a frequent crafter, you'll find lots of occasions to use it. **Tip for use:** The product comes with a plastic squeegee meant to be used to smooth and press the adhesive to create firm and complete coverage. I found the squeegee to be nearly worthless, leaving bare spots and weak bonds. I rolled my projects with a brayer to achieve the bond I wanted. If you don't have a brayer, a heavy wine bottle or another smooth, heavy cylinder will work well.

8

Stickles™ Glitter Glue by Ranger. There are a few glitter glues out there, but Stickles is my favorite. The glitter glue itself is sparkly and comes in wonderful shades, but an even more impressive feature is the container it comes in. It's easy to hold, with a nozzle so fine you can draw with it, make tiny dots like the ones on the Snowflake Wrapping Paper on page 105, or embellish small, finely detailed areas. It's also extremely forgiving: if you make a blob where you meant to make a dot, quickly scrape up the excess, blot the damp spot with a tissue, and let it dry. Most of the time, you'll get away with it. **Tip for use:**

To outline details like folds in fabric, apply a short, thin line of Stickles, and then use the point of a bamboo skewer to drag the glitter glue along the lines you want to highlight. **And a word of advice:** Stickles often looks and feels dry when it really isn't, and can smear. Always set your work aside to dry overnight before going further on your projects.

Terrifically Tacky Tape® by Provo Craft. When you need a really strong bond and a product that sticks to almost anything, this is the product to use. I've tried it on plastic, glass, Styrofoam, paper, and candles, all with good results. It grabs and holds tricky substances like glitter and tiny beads well without the mess of glue, meaning you can brush away the excess without damaging your project. I've even tried to scrape glitter off a piece of it, and was happy to discover I couldn't. The tape is positionable, giving you an opportunity to correct mistakes, but once the bond takes, it's there to stay. **Tip for use:** Terrifically Tacky Tape is covered with a liner, which is eventually peeled away. Since the tape widths are narrow, separating the liner from the tape can be a bit frustrating. The easiest way is to hold the tape with the sticky side facing you and use the point of a straight pin to dig between the tape and the liner. Peel away 1/4" so of the tape, snip it off, and discard. You've now created a nonsticky tab of liner to use. Instead of struggling when it's time to expose the sticky tape, you can just pull the liner tab and peel it away.

CHAPTER 1

From Dickens to Deco: The 1920s

For sheer change, it would be hard to find another decade quite like the '20s. It started with the ring of a cash register and raced along like quicksilver. American cities glowed with electric lights, women flaunted short hair and shorter skirts, the air filled with voices that anyone with a radio set could hear for free, and people born in Minsk or Naples or ten thousand other places landed in Brooklyn and rooted for the Dodgers like their lives depended on it. Nothing was as it had been.

Except for Christmas.

For all the innovations, Christmases of the 1920s looked remarkably traditional, perhaps because the country's bare-kneed, bobbed-hair daughters were out dancing, leaving the decorating to Mom and Dad. Yet even among the most jaded of the Lost Generation there was no real desire to modernize Christmas as rapidly as they were modernizing their lives. Some hallmarks of 1920s Christmas style include:

• **Paper.** Paper decorations were extremely common throughout the '20s, even in the most upscale of homes. One of the most popular items was a **red honeycomb bell**, most often fixed to the center of the ceiling, with **crepe paper streamers** radiating from the bell to the far corners of the room. We once saw a picture of a nursery in a wealthy home that had its own honeycomb ceiling bell, and even the crib was decorated with crepe paper streamers. Other popular paper decorations included **tissue paper garlands** for the mantel and **German die cuts**.

• **Colors.** Throughout the '20s, there was less emphasis on traditional Christmas colors than in most other decades, and ornaments and cards were more likely to sport the era's most fashionable colors—pastels. At the beginning of the decade, the shades were soft and romantic—**lavender, pale robin's egg blue, cream, rose**. But as the pace of the decade accelerated and art deco began to filter into the mainstream, the pastels became more opaque and intense, losing their misty watercolor quality and foreshadowing the **hot pinks and vivid aquas** of another anything goes decade, the '60s. Nevertheless, if there was a single dominant color for Christmases of the '20s, it was red. Not red and green, but red. When green appeared, it was usually depicting holly or evergreens. It was seldom translated, as red was, into other decorations. Red was the color for bells and bows, for stockings hung by the fire, table runners and mantel scarves, and wide satin ribbons encircling gifts wrapped in white tissue.

• **It's the Dickens!** After the shock of World War I, people craved the comfort of more innocent times. They found it in the world of Charles Dickens. There were four different film versions of *A Christmas Carol* to choose from, and magazine covers of the era often depicted scenes with the flavor of merry old England. While people couldn't physically go back to that idyllic past, they could bring bits and pieces of it into their homes. **Carriage lanterns** became a popular motif, English **holly** was more popular than American pine, and mantels featured **candles in antique holders** of the sort Wee Willie Winkie might have used to light his way up the stairs. Also popular were **silhouettes**, a parlor art that began in France in the 1700s and reached its golden age in England during Dickens's time.

• **Hearth and Home.** Unlike decades that saw Christmas as a holiday of nonstop socializing, the '20s emphasized its snug, **homey coziness**. Endless greeting cards show cottages and villages nestled under thick eiderdowns of snow or couples sitting peacefully before the hearth. In fact, **mantels and hearths** are about the only interior parts of the home shown on cards of the era, far outnumbering depictions of even the tree itself.

• **Children and Toys.** As icons go, **children were more popular than Santa**, appearing on far more holiday cards and in countless magazine illustrations. Unlike the stiff, somewhat posed children of earlier decades, '20s children were shown in more natural settings. Snow Baby figurines, imported from Germany, were especially popular. One of the unique and charming customs of the '20s was using **toys as decorations**. The toys were not new or specially bought, but belonged to the children of the house, who must have had a hand in choosing their favorites to arrange in elaborate vignettes.

• **The Dawn of Deco.** Art deco caught on much more quickly in Europe than it did in the United States. Yet, by the end of the decade, its outlines could clearly be seen. Its curving lines accented otherwise traditional **greeting cards**, and **wrapping paper** suddenly appeared in bold geometric patterns, such as harlequin diamonds in black and gold, with **gift tags** and cord to match.

What You Won't See: The Case of the Poisoning Poinsettia

The beautiful, showy, oh-so-Christmasy poinsettia, today America's best-selling potted plant, was seldom seen during the 1920s. People believed the plant was poisonous, due to a story that a child died shortly after eating one of its leaves. Although the belief was false and the plant is nontoxic, it took more than a decade for it to become a common yuletide decoration.

To Make a '20s Tree

Trees of the '20s were round and fat, so full that to get the desired girth people often bought a tree that was taller than the room it was intended for and lopped off the top. The practice was so common that tree toppers played no part in many homes, nor did lights, which were expensive and consumed large amounts of electricity. Despite the lack of lights, trees of this era had impressive dazzle and a distinctive charm all their own.

Balls and glass ornaments were less numerous but more distinctive than those of today. Almost all had been hand-cast and hand-painted in Germany, and were sold as expensive individual items rather than by the box or the dozen. Popular shapes included **globes and teardrops** as well as **pinecones, fruit, dogs, cats**, **wild animals**, and **figures such as Santas**. Families often bought one ornament a year, and it could easily take a generation to accumulate a collection. Because of this, each ornament was given a prominent position on the tree, even ordinary balls, which were sometimes wrapped in threads of gold cord or suspended in ribbon cradles.

Families looking for ways to augment their collection of glass ornaments found many inventive ways to do so.

Papier-mâché ornaments, painted and often embellished with cloth, ribbons, beads, or glitter, added a rich, full look to the tree. Especially popular were **birds, bells,** and **elves**. **Small toys** belonging to the children were occasionally added, as well as treasured but outgrown **baby shoes**.

Die-cut images. Large, lavish die-cut images printed on heavy cardboard and embellished with embossing, gilt, and sometimes crepe paper like the Medallions project on page 23, were a hallmark of early-twentieth-century trees. They offered a potpourri of themes and colors, though few were tied explicitly to Christmas. **Lucky horseshoes, Irish harps, shamrocks, Uncle Sams, Lady Liberties, old-fashioned high button shoes, and hands holding nosegays** were seen on many trees, making them the subject of endless fascination.

Treats. Have you ever wondered why Animal Crackers have a string on the box? Originally these small boxes were meant to hang on Christmas trees. The custom of putting children's treats on the tree, widespread in Europe, was eagerly embraced in America and, as mass production and packaged food became more widespread, **small boxes of purchased treats** gradually replaced the paper cones of Victorian times.

Garlands. The sparkle trees lacked before lights became common was more than made up for by an **abundance of garlands**. One or two were never enough, and it isn't unusual to see trees sporting four, five, or even six of them, with no two alike. Some were made of **papier-mâché balls**, painted or gilded and dusted with glitter. More expensive garlands used **large glass beads similar to small ornament balls**, the luxurious rounds separated by long tubes and smaller beads to keep costs within reason. Also popular was **lametta**, a thin wire covered with short, tinsel-like projections that caught the light and sparkled like tinsel. As a final touch, **golden thread or cord** was also swagged liberally among the branches, giving the whole tree the look of being held in a fretwork of shimmering gold.

Beneath the Tree

One of the most charming aspects of a '20s tree was often what lay beneath it. Piling wrapped packages there does not seem to have been the custom, as it is today. Instead, tiered risers were arranged around the trunk, a sheet was spread over them, and a **landscape in miniature** was created. All the children's smallest toys—boats and farm animals, Noah's arks and milk trucks and pieces of dollhouse furniture—were drawn into the effort. Adults clearly had a hand in the effort, as can be seen in the elaborate and detailed appearance of blue rivers and grassy meadows, but children must have had a part as well, and the staging was probably as much looked forward to as the finished project was.

Get the Look

Despite the era's reputation as one of decadence, meteoric rises, and cavernous falls, there was an underlying sweetness that shone forth in Christmases of the '20s, and an exuberance of style that is well worth preserving. Here are some ways to recapture the look and spirit of those times.

• Move the packages to the side and replicate a miniature landscape of villages, pastures, and farms beneath the tree. These tableaux were one of the era's most charming features, and you should not miss the fun of creating one with your family. If the space beneath the tree isn't a practical location, look for low-lying venues such as a fireplace ledge, low bookshelf, or even a coffee table. My theory is that these stagings were always placed at child-height to keep the children playing and preoccupied, minimizing any temptation to plunder closets and cupboards in search of hidden presents. **Tip:** If the toys in your house look a little too modern, there are wonderful sets of '50s and '60 farm animals on eBay that will do the trick for a reasonable price.

• Replace the usual pine with holly, and instead of adorning your door with an evergreen wreath, try a spray of holly tied with red ribbon. (Use artificial holly if you have children or pets, as the real thing is toxic if ingested.)

• Make red the dominant color, rather than mixing red and green. Make a red table runner, choose red candles, find a large red velvet bow for the newel post at the bottom of the stairs. The colored dishes that came to be known as Depression glass were first made in the '20s, so a red glass candy dish would be a perfect addition to your living room. Since green wasn't particularly popular at this time, try white or cream as a contrast color.

• If your home has a fireplace and mantel, make it the focal point, just as they did in the '20s. Dress the mantel with candles and holly or swag it with a garland.

• Replace pillar candles with tapers displayed in old-fashioned holders like candoliers or the Wee Willie Winkie–style candleholder mentioned earlier.

• Look for inexpensive straight-sided battery-lit lanterns to adorn the mantel or bookshelves. You can also mass midget lights in a lantern and hide the telltale cord with twinings of holly and ivy.

• You may not want a large honeycomb bell dangling from the ceiling, but smaller red bells placed in doorway arches can be quite cheerful.

• Use small artificial birds as tree ornaments. All the better if they come in pastel shades and have beaded tails like the ones in the 1960s wreath on page 99. If your birds don't come with clips, you can wire them to branches.

• When Department 56 began manufacturing the small, charming figurines known as Snow Babies in the 1980s, most people assumed they were a new and thoroughly modern item. Although the figurines were original rather than reproductions, Snow Babies were manufactured in the early decades of the twentieth century and remained popular in the '20s. Today's figures are similar in style as well as spirit to the best of the earlier items, and suggest the era's fondness for its children.

• The '20s were preceded by an era of mass immigration, and memories of home and family left behind were still fresh in the minds of many. If you are lucky enough to have keepsakes handed down from immigrant ancestors, Christmas is an ideal time to give them pride of place, and thoroughly in keeping with how Christmas was celebrated during that decade.

Crafts

ORIGINAL WRAPPINGS

Considering the fact that gift giving began with Christmas itself, it took a remarkably long time for gift wrap to make its way onto the scene. Turn-of-the-century gifts came in white pasteboard boxes or boxes printed with holly sprigs. White, holly-sprigged tissue paper arrived early in the first decade of the century, and by the early 1920s you could buy it with a choice of red or green sprigs, to be held in place by gummed seals that never worked as well as they were supposed to. As for the era of "brown paper packages tied up with strings," *strings* was the operative word. Except for an occasional flash of red satin ribbon, most packages were tied with cord or twine, similar to the easy-to-make, inexpensive butcher's twine shown at right. Conveniences like cellophane tape, curling ribbon, and press-on bows were all still a decade or more away.

MATERIALS FOR HOLLY SPRIG PACKAGE:

Holly sprig mini-stamp:

Red ink pad

White paper and red ribbon

Materials for striped butcher's twine:

6-strand embroidery floss in red and white,

or any two colors of your choice

Spray starch and iron

How to make holly sprig package:

Create gift wrap by randomly stamping holly sprigs on plain white paper. Tie with red satin ribbon and, for a truly authentic touch, hold wrappings in place with seals made using the directions on page 31.

Tip: The best thing to make wrapping paper from is wrapping paper. Buy inexpensive rolls of wrap at the discount store and use the blank side as your canvas.

How to make butcher's twine:
Cut a piece of 6-strand embroidery floss long enough to wrap your package and tie a bow.

Cut an equal length in a second color. Submerge each length in water for a few moments to thoroughly dampen. Squeeze out the moisture. Bring the ends together and make a slipknot.

Fasten the slipknot over a doorknob or anything else that will hold it in place while you work. Draw one length taut and wind the contrasting color around it, candy cane–style. Do this all the way to the end of the floss. Make a slipknot and secure it by taping it to something or looping it over another doorknob.

Set your twine by ironing it with spray starch. Always knot and anchor the ends to prevent fraying and discourage untwisting.

MEDALLIONS

Medallions were a common decoration of the era, and a good example of the many showy, festive paper decorations favored at this time. Though circular shapes were the most common, diamond shapes also make attractive centers. **Note:** Because glitter glue needs to dry several hours or overnight, this is a two-part project. These directions are for the sledding dogs medallion shown. If you choose a different image, coordinate colors accordingly.

MATERIALS:

Two copies of the sledding dogs medallion image on page 124

Sheet of crepe paper in an off-white shade (The medallion shown uses French Vanilla from Blümchen. Streamer-style crepe paper in a roll will not work for this.)

Stickles Glitter Glue in gold, red, emerald, and white

Terrifically Tacky Tape, ¼" width

3" square of lightweight cardboard, such as from a cereal box

16" length of ribbon

Double-sided tape

How to:

Cut out medallions and set aside. Cut a strip of crepe paper 30" long by 1¾" wide. Make sure the grain of paper runs the short way. You want it to look like it's radiating from the center of the medallion.

Squeeze a small drop of gold glitter glue onto the edge of the crepe paper strip and spread it with your fingers. Repeat this process all the way to the end, so there are flashes of glitter along one edge the entire length of the strip. Set this aside to dry.

Use green, red, and white glitter glues to highlight the holly leaves, berries, and mounds of snow on each medallion. These will take longer to dry than the crepe paper. Because you'll be handling them to complete the project and will want to avoid smearing, we recommend letting them set overnight.

By the time you finish decorating the images, check to see if the glitter on the crepe paper is dry. When it is, turn it over and glitter along the back side of the first edge you did.

When all the glitter is dry, you're ready to complete your project. Place one of the images facedown on a clean piece of paper. Mark 1/2" in from the edge all the way around. This is your placement guide for the tacky tape. Attach the tape to a marked spot and adhere a few inches, following the inner circle you have marked. Peel back the liner and begin attaching crepe paper along the unglittered edge, scrunching in tiny gathers as you go and pressing firmly to the tape.

Continue going, a few inches at a time, all the way around. You do not need to cut the tape from the roll unless you've gone off track and feel you need to reposition. Plan to end up with a few inches of extra crepe paper.

When you've gone all the way around, overlap the edges of the crepe paper. Cut the tape and crepe paper and set aside the leftover piece.

Cut a 2 1/2" disk from the square of cardboard. Cut the ribbon in half and use tacky tape or double-sided tape to attach the end of each piece to the cardboard disk. Attach one piece to the front side and the other to the back in exactly the same place.

On the wrong side of the image you have just attached the crepe paper to, make a pencil mark to indicate the top center of the image. Cover one side of the cardboard disk with double-sided tape and attach it to wrong side of the image, within the edges of the crepe paper and with the ribbons aligned to the top center mark. Press firmly and set aside.

Now mark 1/2" in from the edge on the back of the remaining image for a few inches around the top. Use tacky tape and a bit of the leftover streamer to cover this short curve, again scrunching the paper to make a ruffle. This is only to cover the ribbon and keep your medallion from having an obvious "back."

Cover the exposed side of the cardboard disk with double-sided tape, position the image with its short frill of ruffle to align, and press firmly to adhere.

You now have a beautiful and perfectly authentic medallion.

CHRISTMAS POSTCARDS

Christmas cards remained a novelty throughout much of the decade, and many people preferred sending postcards as they always had. Whereas cards were printed on thin paper folded into quadrants, a postcard printed on cardboard or heavy card stock often seemed more opulent, with brighter colors, finer detail, and added touches like embossing or gilt. And wasn't the picture really what it was all about?

MATERIALS:

Postcard image and postcard back from pages 122 and 123,
  or images of your own
Stickles Glitter Glue
Scotch Positionable Mounting Adhesive or double-sided tape
Cardboard trimmed to the size of the card (An empty cereal
  box works well.)

How to:

Photocopy or scan and print the postcard back and image. Cut out and set aside.

Cut a piece of cardboard to fit. Use mounting adhesive or double-sided tape to adhere the front and back card pieces to the cardboard. For how-tos on Positionable Mounting Adhesive, see page 8.

After the postcard is assembled, select areas of the card to highlight with glitter glue. Snow and snowflakes are always good glitter, as are edges of clothing, holly berries, evergreens, and the tips and edges of birds' wings. You want a little sparkle, not a lot. For how-tos on using Stickles Glitter Glue, see page 8.

Variation: Make a hanging for the tree or wall by piercing the cardboard in each upper corner, forcing the ends of a length of 1/8" ribbon through each hole, and taping firmly in place before adhering the front and back postcard pieces.

GLITTER GARLAND

Throughout the 1920s, a tree with only one or two garlands was severely underdressed. Multiple garlands were the hallmark of a '20s tree, with strands of various styles layered on as opulently as the grandes dames of the Gilded Age layered on their pearls. Sparkling lametta crisscrossed with strings of glass crystals or strands of multicolored beads hung in loops so lavish they dipped nearly to the floor. Some strands sported beads the size of today's Christmas balls, while others were thin filaments of spun gold. The final effect—a fretwork of opulent dazzle—would be enough to make you say, "Let's leave the lights off, just this one year, and let the garlands star."

MATERIALS:

Unfinished 12-mm wooden beads, 100 beads for every 4 feet of garland
Glitter in your choice of colors (I used Martha Stewart Crafts
   glitter in Rose Quartz, Blue Topaz, Smoky Quartz,
   and Aquamarine Crystal.)
Bamboo skewers, an old shoebox, ordinary white glue or crafts glue,
   a small brush
Crochet thread and a tapestry needle for stringing

How to:

Pour some glitter into a bowl.

Paint a wooden bead with glue. The easiest way to do this is to slide the bead onto a wooden skewer, hold it upright, and use your thumb to keep the bead from sliding as you apply the glue.

Roll the bead around in the glitter to coat, and let it sit while you do more. When you have several finished balls, thread them onto a clean skewer and set the skewer across a lidless shoebox. Push the balls apart so they aren't touching, and allow to dry at least twelve hours before stringing.

TREAT BOXES

Treat boxes filled with nuts, small candies, and other goodies delight both children and adults and can be used as tree ornaments or party favors. But why go to the trouble of making your own boxes when there are so many forms ready-made for you available for free? The treat boxes in this photo began life as a cream cheese box and a box of bar soap. I've also used butter boxes, pudding and gelatin boxes, boxes staples come in and, of course, the box that inspired it all, the Animal Crackers box.

MATERIALS:

Appropriately sized boxes
Decorative papers
Images, trim, tie-ons, or other decorations
Ribbon
Scotch Positionable Mounting Adhesive
Paper piercer or small, sharp-pointed scissors
Steak knife, craft knife or scissors, double-sided tape, glue dots,
   bamboo skewer

How to:

Use a steak knife to open up the box, sliding it gently under the flaps where they have been glued shut.

Place the flat, opened box on a mat, printed side up. Cut a piece of mounting adhesive large enough to cover the opened box. Position it over the box with the exposed sticky side down and the protective liner up. Press down firmly, smoothing with your hands. It's important to get good and complete coverage, so please see page 8 for how-tos on getting a firm bond.

When you are satisfied that the adhesive is firmly in place, use a craft knife or scissors to trim off the excess.

Make sure the paper you want to cover the box with is large enough. If it isn't, you can patch in a second piece along one of the fold lines. When you've worked out your paper strategy and decided how you want to align the paper (horizontal, vertical, etc.), peel off the liner and affix the paper. When you have a good bond, trim away the excess paper.

Reassemble the box, using double-sided tape to seal all the flaps except the one you want to be the opening.

Make a small mark on each side where you want to attach the ribbon. Pierce the box from the outside, then use the point of the bamboo skewer to gently enlarge the hole. Use the point of the skewer again to poke the end of the ribbon through the hole. Knot the ribbon on the inside. Attach ribbon to the other side of the box in the same way.

Now the fun part—decorating each box to make it one of a kind. Use vintage images, beads and crystals, glitter, and all the exciting scraps left from other projects. One of these boxes uses a length of sequins left over from the Sequined Balls project on page 101, and the other sports a resized vintage postcard.

After you've filled your treat box, use a glue dot to fasten the closure.

All sincere good wishes
for Christmas and the coming Year.

Quick Crafts

Here are some more quick and easy crafts to give your Christmas a '20s touch.

PACKAGE SEALS. No one really wants to go back to a world without adhesive tape, but you can give your package a true '20s look by adding package seals as decorations. Scan or photocopy the seals found throughout the Art Portfolio at the back of this book and apply them to Scotch Positionable Mounting Adhesive (see page 8 for how-to tips). When ready to use, cut out the seal, peel away the liner, and adhere the seal to the package.

SILHOUETTES. Silhouettes were extremely popular throughout the '20s. Find seasonal images that would make good silhouettes and use tracing paper to outline them. Since silhouettes were often small and hung in groups, you may not need to resize them. Use double-sided tape to fix a traced outline to jet-black card stock and cut out your silhouette. Adhere the silhouette to card stock in the color of your choice (cream or one of the Jazz Age's vivid pastels are good options), and frame.

EMBELLISHED ORNAMENTS. Make the most of each Christmas ball by embellishing them as people of the '20s did. Remove the ornament cap, feed a piece of metallic thread through it, attach by knotting to the loop, replace the cap, and wind the thread around the ball at random, changing directions several times to make a crazy quilt net of glistening thread. End by bringing the thread back to the ornament cap. Knot and snip off the stray ends.

NETTED ORNAMENTS. Another way to create a period embellishment for ordinary Christmas balls is to save the stretchy plastic mesh bags onions come in, cut them into squares large enough to contain the ornament, and give them a coat of gold spray paint and a dusting of glitter. When these dry, set a ball in the center and gather the four corners to the top. Secure by tying a loop of gold cord or ribbon just below the ornament cap.

TOYS IN THE TREE. Look for inexpensive toys such as plastic dollhouse furniture, sailboats, and antique-style cars to tuck into the tree. Give them a vintage look with spray paint and a sprinkling of glitter.

greetings

CHAPTER 2

Just Around the Corner: The 1930s

If, in October of 1929, most Americans had been told been told what lay ahead, how long it would last, and that a world war waited on the other side, many would have been tempted to throw in the towel. It was a depression so long it spawned a second slump within the first. Unemployment averaged 18.3 percent for the decade, and the stock market would not retake its 1929 high until 1954, twenty-five years after the Crash. Yet most Americans did not give up. They did what free people do best: They stayed optimistic and made the most of what they had. And no matter how many of their decorations had to be made at home, they still found ways to give the season sparkle.

Many Christmas decorations of the 1930s—especially the expensive ones—were holdovers from the 1920s. When they broke or wore out, they were not replaced in kind, but gave way to something far less costly. Yet people still found ways to make Christmas seem fresh and new, and Christmases of the '30s were as festive as any others, even on a shoestring budget. A key player in all this was Woolworth's. Not only did the famous dime store sell premade decorations for less, but it also fueled a craft boom by selling ribbons, embroidery thread, patterns, fabrics, sequins, glue, and other items at low prices. One could go into the store with little to spend and come out with all the items needed for a Christmas that hit all the right style notes, including:

34

• **Dickens Goes American.** Dickens-inspired landscapes remained popular throughout the '30s but, like all immigrants of long residence, not without changes. Where the '20s celebrated the cozy and sentimental glow of Dickens, the '30s preferred his **grittier and more colorful side**. W. C. Fields's portrayal of the perpetually optimistic and perpetually broke Mr. Micawber in the 1935 film version of *David Copperfield* delighted millions of moviegoers, as did Dickens's **alone-against-the-world heroes**—Oliver Twist, Pip of *Great Expectations*, and Copperfield himself—whose underlying decency and hard work eventually brought them to better times. The image was a perfect fit for America's understanding of its own pioneer spirit. Gradually, English cottages morphed into **American cabins**, snowy villages became **clearings in the woods**, and bushes of English holly became **pine trees** glowing blue in the starlit snow.

• **Children.** Like Dickens, children underwent an update and, because of this, remained popular icons of the '30s. Dickens's rags-to-riches boys spun off American cousins. Shirley Temple became her own industry playing the **adorable, resilient little orphan**. Cartoon character Little Orphan Annie did the same. Child stars like Jackie Cooper and the kids from Our Gang proved their wisdom week after week by getting out of endless scrapes and sticky situations. Children on '20s cards were always portrayed as children removed from the adult world. But children on cards of the '30s often meet your gaze with a high-spirited glance, as if to say, "Yes, we're in a pickle, but we'll get out of it!"

• **Dogs.** Dogs may have figured in more Christmas art of the '30s than in all the rest of human history combined. They weren't the pretty spaniels of the Victorian era nor the languorous borzois and greyhounds of the early twentieth century, nor the sporting dogs of decades to come. No, these were **scrappy little terriers or mutts** with obvious terrier lineage. As with children, such dogs became popular embodiments of the qualities Americans valued in themselves—self-reliance, tenacity, and a certain unsinkable cheerfulness.

• **Colors.** As the glow of the '20s faded, so too did the pastels that marked that era. Sharp times required sharper colors, and the '30s was a decade of **bright primary shades**. The vibrant **red** of the previous decade held on, but now it was paired with equally **vibrant green**. The '30s also went through a **blue** period, and it wasn't uncommon to see entire cards illustrated in nothing but shades of blue and white.

• **Santa.** In 1931, Santa's popularity got a huge boost, when the first of Haddon Sundblom's ads for Coca-Cola appeared. Santa had been around for years, of course, but the European Santa was thin and somewhat frightening, and the pre-Sundblom American version, while rotund, often looked weighed down by his responsibilities. But Sundblom painted **Santa as an overgrown child**, and he was an immediate hit with adults and children alike. Bumper crops of **plaster and celluloid Santas**—with or without sleigh—were produced to adorn mantels and tables, **glass Santa ornaments** were sold, and his image began to appear more often in store signage and in ads.

• **Handmade.** More by necessity than choice, handmade items were very much a part of the '30s look. There was a tremendous boom in **needlework** and fabric arts during this decade, so much so that newspapers included craft ideas in the women's section and printed embroidery and quilt patterns as a Sunday feature to draw customers. Men also pitched in: This was a time when many men had basic carpentry skills, and whittling a reindeer or making a sled for a doll was an enjoyable way to pass the evening

To Make a '30s Tree

Two things revolutionized the '30s tree: the continued spread of electricity and Max Eckardt's Shiny-Brite ornaments. **Lights**, which had been a luxury novelty in the '20s, were seen on more trees every year. This shift wasn't because they were that much cheaper—they weren't; it was simply that people were mad for them. Everyone who had electricity wanted a set of tree lights, and if there was one thing the family was going to splurge on, it would be lights. **Colored lights appeared**, as well as lights in figural **shapes, such as bells, Santas, and angels**. Popular cartoon characters like Popeye and Mickey Mouse also appeared on lights. There were even accessories for lights: lightweight beaded clips to hold them in place and colored reflectors to maximize their glow. To make a '30s tree, there must first of all be light.

The second hallmark of a '30s tree came near the end of the decade, when Max Eckardt established the Shiny-Brite company in 1937. The goal of the business was to create the first mass-produced **glass balls and ornaments**. The venture was a success, and once Americans could buy ornaments by the dozen, Shiny-Brite ornaments became a favorite with all who could afford them.

Mixed in with the new splendors were treasures from the past, handmade paper decorations (often done by the children of the house), and less expensive items like tinsel or angel hair.

Get the Look

The '30s look had a **homemade touch** that, in today's busy, prepackaged, and ready-made world, has a charm all its own. Here are some ways to mingle the look with your own traditions:

• Decorative paper was a luxury for many in the '30s. Wrap presents to put under the tree in the **funny pages, plain brown or white paper,** or useful items that are part of the gift, such as a hand-embroidered tea towel or scarf.

• Specially purchased ribbon like the red satin of the previous decade was also a luxury. Look for **rayon seam binding**, available on eBay and often sold in fabric shops, to use for **trimming packages** and tying ornaments on the tree. The colors are vintage, and the ribbon's soft drape is lovely.

• Use embroidered **vintage linen**. Many of us have vintage linen around, pieces made by mothers or grandmothers and now sitting in closets across America. These are the pieces that would have been worked on for months to dress up the Christmas dinner table, so make use of them. If there were no needlewomen in your family, estate sales and eBay are great places to find items at reasonable prices.

• **Depression glass** was at its peak of popularity in the '30s, and green was among the most popular colors it came in. Often, you can buy wonderful authentic pieces like **candy dishes, bowls, relish trays**, and **platters** for less than you would spend on a comparable new item.

• Outdoor lights weren't common in the '30s, yet people wanted to create a Christmasy look visible to passersby. Many homeowners decorated their windows with **swags of pine** or twisted red and green **crepe paper streamers**.

• Instead of angel hair, the skin-irritating spun glass fluff used to decorate trees and mantels in the '30s, try buying cotton batting meant for stuffing and pulling it into loose clumps to create ethereal **drifts of snow**.

• Leaded **tinsel**, so hazardous to the environment, will never be seen again. But in searching for a substitute, I stumbled across something called Flashabou, a sporting goods product meant for tying flies. Made of Mylar, it comes in a host of dazzling, highly un-fishlike colors and is packaged in hanks of 10" lengths. Saltwater Holographic Flashabou in silver is the closest thing I've seen to tinsel in years. Be sure to look for the Saltwater variety, as it's advertised as "wide cut" (1/16") and less fluttery than other Mylar.

Crafts

TREAT CUPS

Not even the Great Depression could completely squelch frivolity in the '30s. The paper party decorations popularized by companies like Dennison and Beistle were still very much in evidence, especially at holidays. Unlike most party favors of today, these weren't just for children—adults also enjoyed the riddles and paper hats, and dug just as eagerly into treat cups filled with mints, burnt Spanish peanuts, and small candies.

MATERIALS:

Crepe paper sheets (streamer rolls will not work)

Tinsel garland

12" tinsel or chenille pipe cleaners, one for each handle,
    plus more for decoration

Small cans, empty and clean (I used 3-ounce cat food cans)

Cupcake wrappers

Terrifically Tacky Tape, $\frac{1}{2}$" and $\frac{1}{4}$" widths

Decorations: charms, tie-ons, small balls and bells

Adhesive tape

How to:

Cut an 11" length of pipe cleaner for each cup. Use ordinary adhesive tape to temporarily tack the handle into position on the outside of the can, ends flush with the bottom.

For each cup you want to cover with tinsel garland, cut a length slightly longer than the circumference of the can (in this case, about 8"). Wind a band of $\frac{1}{2}$" Terrifically Tacky Tape around the can at the center, pressing firmly over the handles. (See notes on using Terrifically Tacky Tape on page 9.) Leave the liner on. Discard the temporary tape, cut two more short pieces of tacky tape, and secure the handle ends to the cup. Remove the liner from all three pieces of tape. Attach the tinsel garland to the exposed tacky tape, trimming off any extra length.

For each cup you want to cover with crepe paper, cut a strip 2 1/2" by 20". Make sure the grain of the paper will be vertical when positioned on the can. Wind a band of 1/2" Terrifically Tacky Tape around the can at the bottom, pressing firmly over the handles. Leave the liner on. Now wind a 1/4" band of tape around the can at the top, just below the rim, again pressing firmly over the handles. Discard the temporary tape. Remove the liner from the tape at the bottom. Attach your crepe paper strip and wind it around the can, scrunching it in tiny gathers as you go and pressing it firmly onto the tape. Cut off any excess. Remove the liner from the upper band of tape and adhere the crepe paper. Gently stretch the top edge of the crepe paper to create a ruffle.

Now the fun part—decorating each treat cup to give it an individual look. These have tinsel pipe cleaner belts and are embellished with package tie-ons (see page 65), Santa jingle charms from Etsy, small plastic bells painted with nail polish (see page 68), and bits and pieces from other leftovers.

Other ways to embellish include edging the crepe paper with glitter glue before attaching, affixing small pieces of seasonal confetti (Christmas trees, snowflakes, snowmen) or punchies (stars and holly leaves) with glue dots, using 1/4" ribbon instead of tinsel belts, and adding press-on crystals.

Before filling with treats, line each cup with a cupcake wrapper.

TREE LIGHT-REFLECTORS

Although tree lights were introduced at the end of the nineteenth century, they remained a luxury for many through the '30s. As late as 1939, 75 percent of those who lived in rural areas remained without electricity, while city dwellers who had it found the lights expensive to purchase as well as to operate. A string of twelve to sixteen lights cost more than $30 by today's reckoning, and were far more expensive to operate than today's energy-efficient bulbs. It's no wonder that those who had lights wanted to make the most of them, perching them on beaded clips and adding colorful reflectors to make each and every light stand out. Early reflectors, made of tin, were soon replaced with lighter, shinier aluminum and clear, hard plastic halos, rimmed and dusted with glitter to maximize the glow.

MATERIALS:

1 or 2 clean, dry 2-liter soda bottles, with the label sleeve removed

Glitter in your choice of colors

Any hard circle, about 1½" in diameter, you can trace around, such as a lid, silver dollar, or cookie cutter (I used the base of a small snow globe.)

Craft knife, utility scissors, brush, and clear-drying glue, such as Mod Podge

How to:

Trace your circle onto a piece of paper and mark the center. Set aside.

Cut away and discard the top and bottom of the soda bottle. Cut open the remaining cylinder so you have a smooth sheet of plastic.

Place the plastic sheet, curved side down, on a cutting mat or thick magazine. Place your hard-edged 1½" circle on it and hold it firmly in place while tracing around it with the craft knife. You aren't trying to cut out the circle, merely score the outline. Trace a circle for each reflector. Line each circle up over the circle you traced on paper and mark the center.

Cut the circles out with utility scissors and use the craft knife or small scissors to cut a 1/2" cross in the center of each disk.

Paint each disk with glue and sprinkle with glitter. If you want a halo effect, dip the edges of the disk directly into the glitter.

Let these dry for twenty-four hours. Mount on midget lights by sliding over the bulb with the curved side facing you. Push gently over the base of the light so the reflector is resting on the base, not the bulb itself.

GOLD TREE-TOPPER STAR

With or without lights, the custom of adding a dazzling topper to the tree was common during the '30s. Various tree toppers have waxed and waned in popularity over the years, with choices that included inverted teardrop ornaments, angels, and stars. During the '30s, as anyone who's watched *It's a Wonderful Life* knows, a star often carried the day.

MATERIALS:

3 yards of stiff mesh ribbon, ⅝" wide (I recommend buying a little extra, in case you make a measuring mistake.)
Craft glue and straight pins

How to:

Cut the ribbon into twelve 9" lengths. This star is made of two identical parts, each using six of the strips.

To make the first half of the star, gather six of the strips and set the rest aside.

Lay one strip down vertically and position a second strip horizontally on top of it so the middles meet to form a cross that is equal on all sides. Adhere the strips together with a drop of glue. Use straight pins to hold this in place while you continue to work.

Lay down two more vertical strips, one on each side of the center strip. The two new strips will lie on top of the horizontal strip. Align the new strips evenly with the center vertical strip and adhere them to the horizontal strip. (See illustration on next page.) Again, use pins to hold the new strips in place as the glue dries.

Take the last two strips for this half of the star and weave one into place on each side of the center horizontal strip. Align them with the center strip and glue each one to the vertical strips below it.

You now have three vertical strips and three horizontal strips that form a perfect basket weave at the center.

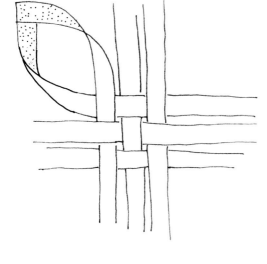

Bend the outermost vertical strip down and away from you, so the underside of the upper part of the strip faces you. Do the same with the horizontal strip nearest it, overlapping the ends to form a point, the undersides of the both strips facing you, as shown in the illustration. Glue the strips together at the point and pin in place.

Repeat with the three remaining corners. The center horizontal and vertical strips will remain unattached.

The first half of your star is now complete. Make the second half in exactly the same way. Allow both halves to dry completely before you remove the pins.

You are now ready to join the two halves together. Lay one half of the star down so the side that was originally facing you is facing down and the basket weave center appears as a diamond. Lay the other half on top of the first so the side that was originally facing you is up and the points of one star are between the points of the other. The basket weave center of the star facing you will appear as a square, and the free strips of each star will align with the points of the other.

Tuck the end of each free strip inside of the point it aligns with and glue these in place. Ignore the overlap, which will be trimmed away later. Use pins or clips to hold these in place.

When the star is completely dry, trim the overlap from the strips. Weave a length of wire through the basket weave center on the back of the star. Twist the ends of wire around the top of the tree to hold the star in place.

YULETIDE SHELF-EDGER

Almost everyone used shelf paper in the '30s, and paper with a fancy, turned down border was a special treat. Whether you use shelf paper or not, this edger is a quick way to get the look—and you won't even have to rearrange your dishes.

MATERIALS:

Round doilies, 6" in diameter

Christmas-themed scrapbook paper

Double-sided tape

How to:

Cut 4 1/2" rounds from the paper, one for each doily.

Use the double-sided tape to attach the rounds to the doilies. Decide which area of each edger you want to be seen. If there's a horizontal and vertical, establish that as well.

Fold each piece in half, using a bone folder or the handle of a table knife to make a sharp, clean crease.

To use your edgers, arrange them along the front of your shelf so the desired side is visible and the edges of the doilies just touch. If you have shelf paper in place, simply slide the upper half of each edger beneath it. If you don't have shelf paper on your shelves, use glue dots to hold the upper halves in place. When Christmas is over, remove any glue dots and store the edgers for use next year.

MERRY CHRISTMAS DISH TOWEL

During the Depression, people looked for decorations that would also serve a practical purpose. This dish towel might have been enjoyed by the maker, given as a gift, or used as gift wrap, a kind of bonus present concealing a more substantial gift within. The crayon tinting used on the towel harkens back to embroidery kits of the era that came with stamped fabric and parts of the picture tinted to add extra appeal.

MATERIALS:

Blank dish towel

Embroidery transfer pencil

Embroidery thread in red, black, white, and green

Tracing paper

Crayons

Painter's tape, masking tape, or pins

How to:

With tracing paper and transfer pencil, trace over the image on page 126. Align the paper to the image on the facing page and complete the tracing.

Position your traced image facedown on the dish towel and tack it down with tape or pins. Heat an iron and press, following the manufacturer's directions for the transfer pencil.

Now it's time to color your picture. If you've never done this before, I strongly recommend trying your hand with the crayons on a scrap of fabric similar to your towel first. You'll enjoy the project much more once you discover how easy coloring on cloth is. Choose which areas you want to color and begin. For covering larger areas, such as Santa's suit or boots, a worn-down crayon works best. Fresh points are better for details and small areas.

When you've finished coloring, it's time to set the color by ironing. Again I recommend

testing, and I recommend it more strongly than I before. To set the color, heat is required, and a "Cotton" setting may be much hotter on one iron than another. You want to set the color, but you don't want to scorch your towel.

To set the crayon, lay a clean sheet of printer paper on your ironing board cover and lay the towel facedown on top of it. Heat your iron to the coolest end of the Cotton setting and press. Don't use steam, and keep the iron moving instead of pressing long in one place. Initially, some crayon will shed onto the underlying paper. When this stops, your towel should be set.

Complete with embroidery. I used three strands on the "Merry Christmas" and the arc beneath it, and two strands everywhere else.

Quick Crafts

Ready for more? Here are five more ways to give your home a '30s look.

PAPER CHAINS. Paper chains were the decoration of last resort when you couldn't afford anything else. Give the old standby a new twist by replacing old-style construction paper with some of the beautiful papers made today. Incorporate vintage-inspired Christmas papers currently available with foil, glittered paper, and mesh paper.

TINY PINECONES. Prized hand-painted ornaments may have included not only balls and teardrops but shapes like pineapples, clusters of grapes, and pinecones. You can replicate the pinecones by gathering small, immature cones that have fallen before fully opening. Let them thoroughly dry out, then coat with copper metallic spray paint. Wind a bit of clear fishing line around the stem, attach to an ornament hook, and add to your tree.

GLASS ICICLES. These ornaments were popular in the '30s, long before the plastic, glow-in-the-dark style of later years. If you're a beader with a lot of crystals or glass beads of various sizes lying around, string a series of same-colored beads in graduated sizes in a 4" length from smallest to largest. Fasten the small end with a crimp bead and create a loop for hanging at the top. Twenty-four gauge wire from the hardware store works well for this.

FANS. One of the first crafts you ever made was probably pleating a piece of paper, stapling it at the center, and taping the uppermost edges together to make a semicircular fan. They knew the technique in the '30s, too, and fans made of foiled paper were a popular tree decoration. Decorate by attaching vintage images at the center: Santas, peacocks, cartoon characters, cats dancing a Christmas jig, and camels with tasseled bridles will make your tree the most fascinating one on the block.

TINSEL STARS. Bend lametta or tinsel pipe cleaners into five-pointed stars, attach ornament hooks, and add to your tree. Don't freehand the stars, but rather make cardboard templates of different sizes to guide you as you bend. If you need to use more than one tinsel pipe cleaner to form a star, join two by twisting the ends together.

CHAPTER 3

Home and Away—and Home Again: The 1940s

There's nothing like a war to put a depression into perspective. No matter how hard times had been during the '30s, people took it for granted that Christmas would be spent with friends and family. That changed on the morning of December 7, 1941. All of America was suddenly on the move. And when it was time to go home for Christmas, transportation was all but impossible to find. Yet the separation and uncertainty added a heartfelt longing that made Christmas all the more treasured. Peace, when it came, had much the same effect. Everyone who'd come through those years had sworn privately, a thousand times, they'd never take the holiday for granted again. For the most part, they kept their pledge.

World War II changed almost everything about Christmas, both during the war and afterward. Looks that will be forever identified with the war years include:

• **Scottish Terriers.** Dogs were still popular, as they had been in the '30s, but now one breed reigned supreme, seen on everything from cards to wrapping paper—the jet-black Scottie. Not only did the little dog embody the tough and intrepid spirit of America and the Allies, but a famous member of the breed was in the White House. **Fala, President Roosevelt's dog**, went almost everywhere the president did, and was photographed and reported on often enough to become a national mascot.

• **Patriotic Themes.** Throughout the war, patriotic themes and decorations were part of Christmas. Some were overt, such as cards showing **flags** or, more optimistically, servicemen and their girls strolling hand-in-hand through an idyllic, peaceful future. **Bells and stars**, with associations to the Liberty Bell and the flag, also experienced a popularity boost. **Candles in windows** suggested a national vigil, the hope of everyone that those overseas would return safely. Thanks to a new item on the market, the **artificial candle** with an electrical cord, people could have a lit candle, without the danger of fire.

GREETINGS!

• **Colors. Red and green** were dominant Christmas colors throughout the decade, but they now competed with **red, white, and blue**. Ornaments in flag colors didn't exactly go with the traditional look, but no one seemed to mind.

• **Plastic, Cellophane, and Papier-Mâché.** With resources like rubber and tin consigned to the war effort, manufacturers looked to other materials to take up the slack. When paper shortages became the norm, packages were **wrapped in cellophane,** which, though likely to tear, was still stronger than the tissue-thin wrapping paper available. **Bells were made of fused, molded cellophane or painted papier-mâché**, and **fringed tissue paper and cellophane garlands** stood in for metal tinsel. A signature piece of the era was the cellophane wreath, usually in red but sometimes seen in green, and often with an electric candle standing proudly within its circle. **Hard plastic**, which had debuted during the 1930s, was also popular, and manufacturers continued to find innovations for this material. Paint was in short supply, but plastic could be dyed, turning an otherwise colorless item into something vibrant. If you've ever seen **red plastic cookie cutters**, this is the decade in which they originated. Plastic could also be molded in much finer detail than plaster. **Santa's sleigh and reindeer** now had delicate runners and finely pointed antlers. Most important, plastic was translucent and could be lit from within. Put a lightbulb inside a **plastic organ** and set it on the mantel, and you really had something. By the time the war was over, customers had grown used to the new materials, and manufacturers had discovered their advantages. People continued to use their wartime decorations and developed a fondness for them that was tinged with nostalgia. To many youngsters born during the post-war baby boom, plastic and cellophane were the stuff childhood memories were made of. It would never again be an all glass and metal Christmas.

• **Cheerfulness.** Perhaps it was due to Roosevelt's conscious decision to keep America's morale high, or the self-confidence earned by coming through the Depression. Whatever the reason, there was a sense of playfulness on display that was unprecedented. **Humorous cards** spoofed Hitler or the foul-ups of rationing and military protocol. Wrapping paper featured whimsical, almost childlike figures. **Snowmen** were especially popular and were often shown in pairs. **Mr. and Mrs. Snow** appeared on package tags and greeting cards, as salt and pepper shakers, on party invitations and hostess aprons. Also popular was the team that pulled Santa's sleigh. ***Rudolph the Red-Nosed Reindeer*** had debuted during the Christmas season of 1939 and became a recurrent motif during the war. Even though the book couldn't be reissued due to paper shortages, Rudolph's image inspired countless figurines and small toys, and was seen on everything from plates to facial tissue boxes. From the '40s on, no Santa-and-sleigh was complete without a red-nosed leader. After the war ended, the determined cheerfulness of the war years was replaced by genuine optimism, and the jaunty high spirits continued through the rest of the decade.

To Make a '40s Tree

Full-size trees were in short supply throughout the war—not because the government needed spruce but because most of the men who cut the trees were overseas. The shortage caused prices to soar, and families who didn't have a soldier coming home on leave often chose to save their money. Taking the place of full-size evergreens were **tabletop trees**. Sometimes these were young seedlings that had been raised in tubs, sometimes they were artificial **trees made of feathers, net, or chenille**, and sometimes they were made of materials meant to resemble pine, such as the most famous alternative of the era—**bottle-brush trees**. Manufactured from the same stuff—and on the same machines—as toilet bowl brushes, they were smaller than tabletop trees and not meant to be decorated. Most often they were displayed in clusters, arranged like miniature forests with drifts of angel hair snow hiding their bases.

Before the war, **tree ornaments** had been widely imported from Germany and Japan. With the outbreak of hostilities, many people left them packed away, untouched. The Shiny-Brite company, which had pioneered domestic mass-production of ornaments near the end of the previous decade, had no trouble producing enough blank glass pieces to handle domestic demand. There was just one problem: The paint needed to coat the balls, bells, and other ornaments was in short supply. Rather than please a limited number of customers but leave many with no ornaments at all, Shiny-Brite made as many blank

glass ornaments as ever but reduced the amount of paint used. Instead of covering the entire ornament, only a few bands of color were applied. **Banded ornaments** became one of the most recognizable features of the war years and remained in use long after everyone could have replaced them with something showier.

After the war trees became full-size again, and companies that had experienced materials and labor shortages could once again focus on producing decorations. Two innovations from this period left a lasting mark on Christmas. Shiny-Brite perfected a technique it had begun working on before the war, casting ornaments of two thin layers of glass and flowing paint between them. The technique, developed in the nineteenth century, resulted in an unusually lustrous product known as mercury glass, named for its silvery gleam rather than use of actual mercury. Shiny-Brite's **mercury glass balls, ornaments, and garlands** were essential features of a post-war tree.

A major innovation in tree lighting came the year after the war ended, when the first **bubbler lights** appeared. Each light consisted of a small glass candle filled with amber liquid that bubbled when heated by the warmth of the bulb. It wasn't quite like the old-fashioned idea of candles on a tree—it was far better. Children especially were fascinated by watching the bubbles in the small glass tubes, and the lights remained popular into the 1950s.

Get the Look

The war years made the '40s a culturally rich decade whose reverberations shaped Christmases for years to come. When you hear Bing Crosby singing "White Christmas," you're hearing the number one all-time most requested song on Armed Forces Radio. When you make balls the focal point of the tree, you're working off the '40s blueprint. When you dress yourself up on Christmas day and dress packages up with gift tags and tie-ons, you're stepping through traditions that became dominant in the '40s. Here are some other ways to ring in the season:

• Wrap **packages in red or green cellophane**, or **white tissue tied with red and blue ribbons**. The deluxe paper you used to buy has been turned into paperback books for soldiers in the field!

• Instead of a wreath on the door, try a **pine spray with a cascade of bells**. During the war, bells, with their patriotic associations, were popular door ornaments. Look for bells with a shape reminiscent of the Liberty Bell. All the better if you can find them in

papier-mâché or red plastic, since metal was scarce at the time. You can also **give metal bells a vintage look** by painting them with a matte finish cream shade inside and out. Don't forget to put a large red bow at the top of the arrangement.

• A candle burning hopefully in a window was a favorite motif of the era, both during and after the war. Put small **wreaths with candles** (battery operated) in several windows, or an electric **candolier** in a main window.

• Add a **patriotic touch**. It doesn't have to break the Christmas mood. Use star ornaments in red, blue, and silver, or add a few small paper flags to the tree (the size you'd put in cupcakes on the Fourth of July). If you have a candolier, arrange some greenery around the base and weave red, white, and blue striped ribbon through it.

• Find space for a **tabletop tree** and decorate it with **miniature balls and ornaments**. You can also decorate it by tying small bows and attaching them to the branches, or adorning them with the candy cane tie-ons described on pages 65 and 66.

• **Clear red plastic cookie cutters** are still to be found at reasonable prices. Set some out in the kitchen, or tie them to your tree with splashy red bows.

Set the Mood with Song

Radio was the mass medium of the day, and after Pearl Harbor people got into the habit of leaving it on throughout the day to hear the latest war news. What they also heard was some of the greatest Christmas music ever written, including "White Christmas" (1942), "I'll Be Home for Christmas" (1943), "Have Yourself a Merry Little Christmas" (1944), "Let It Snow" (1945), "The Christmas Song" (1946), "Here Comes Santa Claus" (1947), and "Rudolph the Red-Nosed Reindeer" (1949).

$\mathcal{C}\text{rafts}$

CELLOPHANE WREATH

Nothing says '40s like wreaths of bright cellophane. They arrived on the scene during the war, when evergreens were at a premium, but people liked them so well they remained an item well into the '50s. Most of the wreaths were red, but green and clear were also manufactured. An electric candle (usually a silvered cardboard tube with a Christmas light at the top) was the decoration of choice. The wonderfully vintage-looking candle in the wreath on page 61 came from Factory Direct Craft Supply online.

MATERIALS:

One circle from a 12" embroidery hoop, inside or outside

One roll 40" wide cellophane, at least 15 feet long

One battery-lit candle (Don't get one with a holder-type base.
   You want just the candle.)

Ping-Pong ball

Wire, paper piercer or large needle, craft knife, small
   sharp-pointed scissors

How to:

To make this wreath, you will need to cut approximately 225–250 cellophane strips, 2½" x 10" in size. The easiest way to do this is to lay the roll on a table and cut three or four 40"-long crosswise strips. Lay the strips on top of each other and cut into four 10" pieces. Don't cut the ends of the pieces straight across but at a slight angle.

Scrunch three strips together in the middle and tie them around the embroidery hoop with the knot facing you. This will be the front of the wreath. Tie the cellophane to the hoop in bundles of three, cutting more as needed.

When the wreath is full, decide where you want to anchor the candle. If you used the outside circle with the closing screw, you can make that the top and attach a hanging wire from it. Anchor the base of the candle directly across from wherever you want the top to be. To do this, insert the point of a craft knife along the seam of the Ping-Pong ball. Following the seam, cut an incision about 3/4" long. You want to make a cross by cutting a second incision perpendicular to the first. This is easier to do with small sharp-pointed scissors.

Gently push the base of the candle into the ball. You may need to enlarge the slit a bit to make it fit. When the candle end is in the ball, hold the candle upright and press the ball end down on a table so that the bottom of the Ping-Pong ball flattens. Hold the ball and let go of the candle—it should be able to stand straight. Mark which way you want the ball to face on the wreath and remove the candle.

Make two piercings on the right side of the bottom of the ball about ¼" apart; one will be toward the front of the wreath and one toward the back. Make two similar piercings on the left side of the bottom of the ball.

Thread a length of wire into the ball through either of the piercings on the right side, then thread it back out through the other piercing on the same side. Leave a 3" tail of wire extending from both piercings. Repeat on the other side.

60

Push the cellophane ties apart to expose the hoop where you want the candle to be. Place the flattened bottom of the ball on the hoop. To anchor the ball to the hoop, tightly twist the two wire tails on the right side together; then twist together the two wire tails on the left side. Push the cellophane ties back toward the ball and fluff them up to hide the candle base.

BANDED BALLS

Paint shortages were only one of many that resulted from the mass reallocation of wartime resources. As for most other items, an alternative was found for painted ornaments. Blank glass forms were made as they'd always been, but decorated with just a few bright bands to conserve paint. But glitter is even prettier!

MATERIALS:

Plain glass ornament balls

Terrifically Tacky Tape, ¼" and ⅛" widths

Glitter

Gold stars (These came from a bag of laser confetti.)

Small brush, glue dots, bowls

How to make a three-banded ball:

Using the ¼" width of tacky tape, make a belt around the ball where the equator would be. Don't remove the liner. (See page 9 for tips on working with tacky tape.) Try to keep the band of tape even, but don't make yourself crazy—if you look at balls from the era, they aren't perfectly even either.

Apply a band of ⅛" wide tape a bit above the first band and another below the first band, leaving the liners on. Go over each band firmly with your fingers, using your thumbnail to smooth down any bubbles.

Remove the liner on the band you want to glitter. (Even if you are going to do all three bands in the same color, do one band at a time.) Holding the ball over a bowl, pour glitter liberally over the ball. Pour more glitter in the bowl. Roll the ball in the glitter and scoop more over it, until you are satisfied with the coverage. Do the remaining bands the same way. Use the same technique for a five-banded ball.

Set the balls aside overnight. The next day, brush away any excess glitter clinging to the untaped sections into a bowl.

How to make a hit if you're a Miss (or a Mrs.)
give him a STETSON
Gift Certificate

To make the stars and bars ball:

Apply two bands of 1/8" width tacky tape to a blank glass ball, about ¾" apart. (Make sure the space is wide enough to accommodate your stars.) Glitter each band with silver as described on page 62.

Use a glue dot to attach a gold star to the ball in the space between the silver bands. Attach the second star directly across from it on the other side of the ball. Attach the third star between the first two and the fourth star across from it, so the stars form the four points of a compass. Finish by attaching four more stars, one between each of the stars already in place.

PACKAGE TIE-ONS

I mourn the passing of package tie-ons. There was nothing as festive as that little bonus added to the parcel, like the prize in a box of Cracker Jacks. Happily, all it takes to bring back this glorious tradition is a few packs of pipe cleaners and some trinkets.

MATERIALS:

Tinsel pipe cleaners

Bump chenille pipe cleaners, 3" size: red, white, and green

Regular or bump chenille pipe cleaners, black

Leftover red painted bells from the Bell Garland project on
   page 68, or small silver or gold plastic Liberty Bell–style bells,
   ¾" wide

Glitter (optional)

Stickles Glitter Glue, red

How to make little wreaths: Wind a piece of green tinsel pipe cleaner once around the base of your forefinger. Fasten to make a closed circle. Cut off the excess length, leaving a tail to fasten to a package. Add berry clusters to your wreath with drops of glitter glue.

How to make candy canes: Twist a length of red and silver tinsel pipe cleaner together. Form the candy cane's hook by wrapping halfway around a pencil, then trim to the desired length.

How to make a bell tie: Paint the rims of the bells with red or clear nail polish, or gloss with a bit of glue, then dip into glitter. Attach to a bit of tinsel pipe cleaner.

How to make a miniature pine tree: Cut a piece of green bump chenille pipe cleaner in half at its midpoint, where it is the fattest.

How to make a Santa: Cut three bumps of red chenille and one of white. Bend two pieces of the red chenille into U shapes and hook them together, as if they were links in a chain. The bump facing you is Santa's lower half. Twist the arms of the upper U to hold it firmly on the lower U, and pull each arm straight out to the side. Now cut one piece of white chenille. Holding the narrow end to the back, give Santa a white belt by wrapping all the way around. Pull the tail of white chenille straight up, so it emerges between Santa's arms. Bend into a loop to form Santa's head. From the remaining bump of red chenille, form a coil that will fit atop Santa's head. Bend the end of the bump to make a jaunty tail. Bend or glue bits of black chenille to the tips of the lower U to form Santa's boots. Finish Santa by placing a candy cane in one hand and a chenille Christmas tree in the other.

BELL GARLAND

When the war ended, people were hungry for all the consumer goods that had been unavailable, including Christmas ornaments. Never had people been so grateful for something as simple as ornament hooks or as ready to spend money on something sparkly and new. So pent up was the demand that stores actually ran ads begging customers not to buy too much, assuring them that there would be enough for everyone for years to come. Metal could be used in ornaments once more, and colored metal became especially popular. This rich-looking garland would have satisfied almost any shopper, yet it costs very little to make.

MATERIALS:

Small silver or gold plastic Liberty Bell–style bells, ¾" wide
Bright red nail polish
Clear red glass beads, 6-mm size (Red glass pearls would also work.)
Gold spacer beads, 4-mm size
3 or 4 pencils
Crochet thread and tapestry needle for stringing

How to:

Paint each bell with a thin coat of red nail polish. The easiest way to do this is to put the bell on the eraser end of a pencil, hold the top in place with your forefinger, and rotate the pencil while holding the nail polish brush against the bell. Don't try to apply a thick layer—it's the gleam of gold or silver showing through the polish that gives the finished bell a metallic look. Set the pencil with the finished bell on it in a pencil holder to dry. By the time you've finished three or four bells, the first ones will be dry.

Thread a tapestry needle with cotton crochet thread and start stringing. Use one bell, two red beads, one gold bead, two more red beads, then repeat the sequence to reach the desired length.

GIFT TAGS

After the war, people decided to do Christmas *big*, will all the trimmings. They dressed up for the event, even if it was spent at home. Men wore ties and women put glitter in their hair. Even the packages were better dressed, sporting vibrant paper and gift tags that said more than *To* and *From*.

MATERIALS:

Images on page 125 of this book
Stickles Glitter Glue
Optional additional embellishments
Ribbon
Paper piercer or small paper punch, double-sided tape

How to:

Photocopy or scan and print several copies of the images you want to use, then cut out and finish as you wish. To keep a vintage look, try picking out details and borders in glitter glue. You could also cut the images out with decorative-edged scissors, mount them on slightly larger pieces of card stock with double-sided tape, and decorate the undercard with mini-stamps, confetti, or punchies for a slightly more contemporary look.

Use a paper piercer or a small paper punch to make a hole to thread ribbon through and tie to a package.

Quick Crafts

The war-and-peace decade was so rich I hate to leave it behind. If you feel the same way, here are five more things to make:

LITTLE CHENILLE WREATHS. Cut a flat cardboard donut 3" or 4" in diameter and ½" wide. Wrap regular or bump chenille all the way around in your choice of colors—red, green, white, and baby blue are all good choices. Decorate as you would a full-size wreath. Glue on red bead berries, use silver and gold beads for ornament balls, add a bow with trailing tails. Attach a loop of cord to the back as a hanger.

WRAPPED BALLS. If you made the Cellophane Wreath on page 59 and the Banded Balls on page 62, put your leftover materials to good use. Cut or tear small (about 1") pieces of cellophane. Use Mod Podge Gloss or any other clear-drying glue to cover a clear glass ornament ball with pieces of cellophane, overlapping pieces to create depth and dimension. If you want a second layer, be sure to let the first layer dry thoroughly before adding the second.

SCOTTIES. Honor Fala, the famous First Dog of the '40s, with a tree ornament. Trace or photocopy the Scottish terrier on page 130. Use this as a pattern to cut two pieces of black felt. Stitch a bead on each piece for an eye, then use a blanket stitch and embroidery floss to sew the pieces together, right sides out. Start with legs so that the stomach area will be the last thing you do. When you get there, stuff lightly with cotton batting, using a bamboo skewer to push some into the head and legs. You just want to use enough to give your dog some body. Stitch the belly closed. Finish with a red ribbon collar and a loop of cord or embroidery floss for hanging.

STATIONERY. After the war, people who'd once never known anyone who lived more than a few miles away found they had all sorts of far-flung friends, both people they'd met in the service and hometown friends who had settled in other parts of the country. Christmas-themed stationery became a popular item, and the custom of the annual family update letter began. Try your hand at making your own Christmas stationery. Cut and lay out vintage images from the Art Portfolio at the back of this book. Use double-sided tape to hold your arrangement in place, then take it to a printing company for photocopying and printing, or scan and print from your home computer.

MINIATURE TREE ORNAMENTS. Instead of buying miniature ornaments for your tabletop tree, do what they would have done in the war: *Use it up, wear it out, make it do, or do without.* In other words, make your own ornaments from whatever you have on hand. Your jewelry box is a good place to start: try **pearl or rhinestone necklaces as garlands**, stray **charms** and **beads as ornaments**, and a **sparkly earring** as a tree topper. Originally, doll-size glass cups and teapots were favored ornaments for tabletop trees. Although you can still find pieces from this era at a price, you can save money by buying new **miniature porcelain tea sets**. The size (about 2½" for the teapot) matches the size of vintage items, and there are plenty of pretty styles to choose from. I even found one with a Santa teapot, green holly cups, and a Christmas tree platter. To attach, glue the lid to the teapot and tie a loop of 1/8" ribbon through the handle as a hanger. Hang the cups in the same way. To use the saucers or tiny plates as ornaments, cut the "eye" section of a picture hanger to fit, adhere to the saucer, and run a piece of ribbon through the eye to make a loop-style hanger.

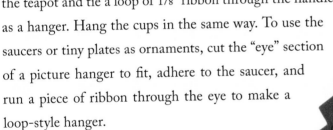

Midcentury Modern: The 1950s

The irony of war is that even if you win, the country you've just fought to save is almost unrecognizable by the time you get back to it. World War II catapulted America from the lingering Depression of the '30s to the hypermodernism of the '50s and '60s. Nothing was as it had been before, but no one seemed to care. The world had been made safe, the Axis had been defeated, and everything was new.

The housing shortage that followed the war was remedied by a building boom that began in the late '40s and lasted well into the '60s. More than five million acres of land were cleared for houses in the '50s alone. With lower ceilings, picture windows, and rooms that flowed smoothly into each other, the new houses bore little resemblance to their predecessors. Decorations that had been designed for the '20s and '30s looked a bit strange in Cape Cods, ranch ramblers, and split-levels. When factories that had been reconfigured for war work returned to commercial production, they turned out new styles suited for the updated way of living. Here are a few of the trends that made Christmas in the '50s different:

• **The Designed Look.** New homes, new styles, and a new prosperity conspired to make Christmas a **far more stylish affair** than it had been in the past. Hauling out the same old decorations year in and year out was no longer acceptable. Homes were now expected to carry off a designed look, with **modern touches in high-fashion colors**. This was an outcome of the new suburban lifestyle, where going out with friends was replaced by entertaining at home. **Bathrooms and kitchens, hallways and rec rooms** all had to be ready for friends who might drop by.

• **Novelty.** To decorate all the rooms of their homes in style, people needed new kinds of **Christmas-themed accessories**—a holly-bordered **doormat** to welcome guests, highball **glasses** with tobogganing snowmen, **matches** that wished you happy holidays while you lit up, and candy cane **hand towels** for the bathroom. The electric candoliers that adorned fireplace mantels in the '40s triggered a craze for **electrically lit tabletop decor**, with items made of hard plastic containing bulbs that glowed from within. **Choirboys, churches, and angels** were among the most popular themes.

• **Focus on the Tree.** Previously, the fireplace mantel had often been the focus of the room, with the tree standing to the side. Modern homes frequently lacked fireplaces or, if they had them, featured low ledges rather than mantels. Without a stocking-bedecked mantel to compete with, the **tree was the most important decoration in the house**, and homeowners often **framed the tree in the picture window** for the whole neighborhood to admire.

• **Colors.** Red and green were still prominent at the start of the decade, but soon blues edged in to become the Christmas trend. **Heavenly blue,** a soft, heavy pastel that was deeper than baby blue and looked as if it might glow in the dark, was especially popular in the early '50s. By the end of the decade, this heavenly blue had transitioned to aqua, and was joined by a new color combination, **pink and charcoal gray**.

• **Poinsettias.** Poinsettias had been gradually gaining ground as a symbol on cards, but during the '50s they **became popular decorations for the home**, their lingering reputation as a poisonous plant finally put behind them. Their newfound prominence was largely the work of a poinsettia-growing family based in California. Albert Ecke and his son had been promoting their poinsettias for decades, but with the coming of television, they saw their opportunity. The Eckes sent plants to television studios for use on shows such as *The Tonight Show* and Bob Hope's Christmas specials. Even viewed in black-and-white, the plants' beauty showed, and people wanted them for their own homes. The poinsettia soon became America's best-selling potted plant.

• **Outdoor Decorations**. With the move to the suburbs came a **boom in outdoor light displays**. Previously, a few modest strings of lights might be seen here and there, but only on more palatial homes. The suburbs put every man in control of his own palace and handed him the switch. Now there were **lights everywhere**—on outdoor trees, garage doors, patio railings, even around the chimney on the roof. And lights were only the beginning. Manufacturers created **molded plastic figures for the yards** of ordinary homes, and soon there were giant candles framing doorways, **Santas** on front porches, and snowy lawns crowded with **Nativity scenes, carolers, and sleighs with reindeer**.

To Make a '50s Tree

The single most-changed decoration of the era was the family tree. The beautiful hand-painted ornaments that had once been imported from Germany and Japan disappeared forever, replaced by American-made Shiny-Brite ornaments. Because the American-made items were relatively inexpensive, **ornament balls became the dominant decoration**. Shiny-Brite turned these out in seemingly great variety, offering **reflector balls** and a shortened version of the teardrop, and using the banding technique they'd developed during the war to paint **solid-hued balls with multicolored, Saturnlike rings**. Another addition was the **screen-printed ball**, which featured a monochrome picture or saying in fine detail, often embellished with **flocking or glitter**. Wise men on camels, Santa waving from his sleigh, fluttering angels, and messages that wished "Joy to the World" made each ornament a wonder.

Lights also changed during the '50s. The classic teardrop-shaped Christmas bulb began to give way to new forms and effects. **Flashing lights** were introduced during the second half of the decade, as were the **midget lights** that have become today's standard. Seeking to meet the decade's demand for novelty, GE introduced **round, colored lights** as well as **ice lights**—round white bulbs that appeared to be covered with crystals of ice or snow.

Finally, there were changes in the tree itself. The short-needled blue spruce lost favor to shorter, plumper, long-needled varieties such as the **Scotch pine and Norway pine**. Yet these assaults on tradition paled in comparison to the chief innovation of the era, the **all-aluminum Silver Pine**, a blinding bombshell of a tree that hit the eye with the force of an aboveground nuclear test. Unfortunately, it could have a similar result if lights were attached to it, electricity and metal being a less-than-ideal mix, so manufacturers supplied a color wheel to go with it, a rotating disk that sat in front of a light and cast alternating shades on the tree.

Get the Look

If you weren't lucky enough to inherit a box of '50s ornaments from your parents, there are still plenty of ways to give a nod to the decade that was, in many ways, the heyday of the twentieth-century Christmas. Here are our favorite strategies:

• The war had set the country in motion, and with so many people living far from friends and family, correspondence took on an added importance—so much so that special displays were often made of them. Clip **Christmas cards** to a swag of ribbon, nestle them in the branches of the tree, or pile them in a basket with a bow and make them part of the holiday scene.

• No one in the '50s fretted over opting for **artificial materials**. They saw aluminum trees and **wreaths that looked like tutus** as fun and fashionable. Don't be afraid to follow suit.

• Take a tip from Elvis and have a **blue Christmas**. Whether you go for the true blue pastels of the early '50s or the cool aquas that came late in the decade, let the color dominate. Add blue bows to wreaths, put two blue balls on the tree for every one in another color, or use only blue lights. It's no accident that when tree lights first became available in just one color during this decade, the choice was blue.

• Another way people achieved the blue look in the '50s was to **tint water with food coloring**. An odd fad of the era was to use **liquor bottles as display pieces**. Having been scarce during Prohibition and all but impossible to obtain during the war, alcohol's availability made it a popular gift in the '50s, and manufacturers obliged by packaging it in elegant bottles and fancy boxes. Ladies of the house kept the bottles, filling them with tinted water to enhance the effect. The widely admired practice was touted by magazines of the day as an easy way to add an elegant touch.

• With picture windows came mirrors in the same size and shape. Framed mirrors fell out of favor, and small mirrors were deemed hopelessly old-fashioned. The modern mirror was a large, unframed rectangle of bright glass, often hung directly behind the sofa or in some other prominent spot. When a home decorating magazine suggested **adding ribbon and a huge bow to make the mirror look gift-wrapped**, the look caught on like wildfire—so much so that a special wide, gold mesh ribbon, made of the newly patented Mylar, was produced to complete the project.

• Flower arranging was popular in the '50s, especially Japanese flower arranging, which embodied the spare-yet-striking look of modernism. Women took courses, then experimented with whatever materials came to hand, including pine boughs at Christmastime. One popular was to **arrange a spray of long-needled pine** so that it curved upward from a shallow bowl, then thread **mercury glass beads** over random needles. This is one decoration that looks as fresh and sophisticated today as it did sixty years ago.

• A midcentury home was **guest-ready at all times**, especially Christmas. For a complete '50s look, make sure there are festive touches in every room. Get out your vintage penguin ice bucket, and don't forget the boomerang-shaped chips-and-dip tray!

Crafts

CHRISTMAS CARD PHOTO HOLDER

In the '50s, season's greetings and photography merged to produce the photo greeting card. Though family photos are the norm these days, the original version was more likely to feature children—the baby boom was in full swing, and parents were eager to show off their tots. The flat, professionally printed cards were tucked into the envelope with page-long family newsletters—undertakings that, in the days before photocopying machines and computers, often meant that the lady of the house spent several evenings at a typewriter. We think our version, based on the nightclub-style photo holders of old, is a much better alternative. By putting the photo on the inside, you don't have to write a message at all, just sign your name.

MATERIALS:

2 blank cards, 5" x 3½"

Photo

Photocopy one of the images on pages 128–129

Stickles Glitter Glue, silver

Scotch Positionable Mounting Adhesive

Adhesive tape, double-sided tape

How to:

Cut out the photocopied image and adhere it to the front of one of the two cards with positionable mounting adhesive or double-sided adhesive tape. For tips on working with mounting adhesive, see page 8.

Cut the other card in half along the fold line. Unless you make a mistake, you will only need one of the halves.

Measure your picture. On the wrong side of the half card, draw a centered window that is 1/4" smaller on each side than your photo. Cut out the window.

Position your photo in the window and tape to the card. Use double-sided tape to adhere the piece with the photo to the inside of the card.

Decorate the frame around the photo with Stickles Glitter Glue. For tips on working with glitter glue, see page 8.

Allow to dry completely before closing the card.

CANDY CANE CANDLE

After the bare-bones Christmases of the Depression and the separations and anxieties of the war years, it took a while for the world to pinch itself and realize that Christmas was back. Once it did, though, there was no holding in the exuberance. Christmas became bigger and brighter than ever before. Factories that had been converted to war production retooled for a booming peacetime economy, producing lavish and innovative decorations to replace what had long since worn out. With renewed emphasis on the home and gracious suburban living came such novelties as seasonal centerpieces, hostess aprons, holiday hors d'oeuvres trays, and Christmas card display trees. Candles, plain and simple wax wands in the '40s, did not escape the creative tide, and no hostess worthy of the name would think of failing to coordinate her tapers with the season and the colors of the moment.

MATERIALS:

10" to 12" white candle, preferably straight-sided or
   with very little taper
Terrifically Tacky Tape, ⅛" wide
Red glitter
Bowl, spoon, and brush

Note: This candle was made and tested with Martha Stewart Crafts Coarse Ruby Glitter, which we found to be nonflammable. Always test your glitter first to make sure there's no sparking or flaring as the candle burns.

How to:

Starting at the base, wind tacky tape up the candle in a continuous spiral. Reposition as you go to keep the spacing between spirals as even as possible. Snip at the top but leave the liner on. Go over the candle, pressing the tape down firmly and flattening any bubbles or wrinkles.

Make a second tape spiral about 1/8" away from the first.

Hold the candle over a bowl, and remove both tape liners at once, several inches at a

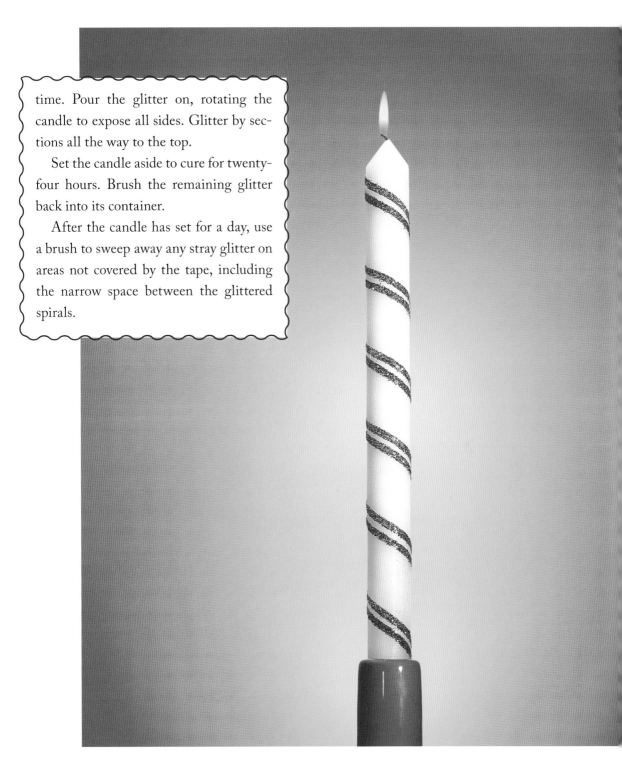

time. Pour the glitter on, rotating the candle to expose all sides. Glitter by sections all the way to the top.

Set the candle aside to cure for twenty-four hours. Brush the remaining glitter back into its container.

After the candle has set for a day, use a brush to sweep away any stray glitter on areas not covered by the tape, including the narrow space between the glittered spirals.

CHRISTMAS MATCHBOXES

These decorative little matchboxes are typical of many '50s-era Christmas accessories—fun, frivolous, and designed to appeal to the host or hostess who wanted to pack every last detail with Christmas cheer. They take minutes to make and are thoroughly at home on any table, even though few people smoke anymore. Remove the matches, fill the boxes with red and green M&M'S, and leave one by each place setting for a sweet and festive update.

MATERIALS:

Photocopies of images on page 131 (You will need a front
   and a back for each box.)
Craft glue and brush

How to:

Cut out the images. Brush the top side of a matchbox with a light coat of glue and adhere the front image. When dry, apply another image to the back of the matchbox.

Note: If you want to make your matchboxes resistant to stains and spills, give the surface a coat of Mod Podge.

PINK WREATH

By the mid-'50s, one of the era's dominant color combinations had come into full flower: pink and gray. Gray Formica sported pink and cream boomerangs. Bathrooms were done in pink wallpaper decorated with poodles and Eiffel Towers in a shade known as French gray, while the number one bedroom theme for girls was toe shoe pink with ballerina wallpaper. There were pink cars, too, and Elvis made his cream-topped pink Cadillac the most famous car in the world. Needless to say, Christmas was not exempt from the passion for pink, and where evergreen wreaths had once prevailed, pink wreaths in feathers, flocking, and frilly tulle now held court.

MATERIALS:

Inside circle of a 12" embroidery hoop

One roll of 6" wide pink net, 40 yards long

35 small Christmas tree balls with caps and loop

    (The wreath shown in picture uses 20-mm silver glittered balls.)

Crochet thread to attach balls to wreath

Note: If you are buying net off the bolt, you need a total of about 60 square feet of net. However, buying by the roll will save you a lot of cutting. I found net by the roll at several sites online, including eBay.

How to:

Cut across the 6" end of the net on a slight diagonal. Measuring from either point cut at the same diagonal to make a 9½" length. Make a second angled piece that is about 6½" long. These will be your templates, so mark with a bit of tape or thread. Since there's a natural tendency to cut larger than the template, using the same template every time will keep your pieces from growing as the project progresses.

    Cut several pieces of each length. You don't need to pin the template on, just lay it over the netting to be cut. When you have a stack of four or five pieces, fold them in half vertically and cut along the fold to make strips 3" wide. Make equal numbers of both lengths. Don't worry if the ends are a bit jagged or some strips are a bit wider than others—it won't make the slightest bit of difference.

Tie the strips to the embroidery hoop, ends equal and the knot facing you on the narrow edge of the hoop. This will be the front of the wreath. Alternate short strips with long ones. You don't need to tie a double knot—one will hold well. And don't worry too much about scrunching or fluffing or getting the spacing just right—the strips will slide enough for you to adjust later.

Continue cutting and tying until the wreath is full, using the entire roll of net. As you near the end, start fluffing and adjusting. Use the last pieces to fill in any area that needs it, and trim off any tails that stick out too far.

Cut two 18" lengths of crochet thread for each of five ball clusters. Thread seven balls onto each double strand and tie tightly to hold the balls in a cluster. Position the clusters evenly around the wreath, about 7½" apart. Pin or tie loosely to the wreath until you're satisfied with the arrangement, then tie each cluster firmly to the hoop with a double knot and trim the ends.

Finish by pulling some of the net around the balls forward to give each cluster a nestled look.

This extremely lightweight wreath doesn't need much to hold it up, and will rest perfectly on a hook on the wall. You can also make a loop of crochet thread, fishing line, or lightweight wire such as florists wire.

ICE LIGHTS

Simply *lighting* a tree has never been quite enough. From the minute tree lights became available, people wanted more—more color, more choices, more dazzle. No sooner had tiny, twinkling midget lights made their way onto the scene than Americans developed a craving for the larger, round globes of earlier years. Frosted glass was a perfect match for the aquas of the late '50s, and manufacturers took the look one step further by affixing icelike crystals to the surface. These Ice Lights pop on over midget lights and can be easily removed and stored in an egg carton when the season is over. Use them with clear lights for a truly wintry look or on colored lights for a soft pastel glow.

MATERIALS

White Ping-Pong balls, one for each light
Colorfill Diamond Vase Filler plastic ice crystals
White or silver glitter
Fine sandpaper
Any white, clear-drying glue that bonds with plastic
  (I used Mod Podge Original Gloss.)
Craft knife, small sharp scissors, pencils, bowl, pencil cup,
  and watercolor brush

How to:

Sand the balls completely to roughen the smooth surface. The glue and crystals will not adhere without this step. When you're finished, the balls should have no trace of shine. Gently insert the point of a craft knife along the seam of a ball. Following the seam, cut an incision about ½" long. You want to make a cross by cutting a second incision perpendicular to the first. This is easier to do with small sharp-pointed scissors.

Pour some of the vase filler into a bowl and keep the rest within easy reach. At the cross, slide the Ping-Pong ball over the end of a pencil. Paint the ball generously with

glue but not so much that it drips. Give the glue a few seconds to set, then hold the pencil and ball over your bowl and pour vase filler on the ball. Dip the ball into the filler in the bowl and keep dipping and rolling until you have loaded the ball. You will not be able to cover the ball completely, and crystals will drop off from time to time, but that's fine—ice crystals don't cover evenly or completely, and that's the look you're going for. When the ball is covered and the crystals are adhering, sprinkle with a little glitter. Prop the pencil in a pencil cup and repeat with the remaining balls.

When you're done, find a place where the pencil cup can sit undisturbed. Although the crystals may appear to be sticking, it takes twenty-four hours for complete drying. After drying, you can touch up any places you feel look too bare, using a small watercolor brush to add more glue and sprinkling on more crystals.

To mount, slide a ball gently over a midget light, pushing until the ball is gripping the cool base, not the warm light.

Christmas Magic

STAMPED RIBBON. One of the more delightful whimsies of the '50s was opaque adhesive tape printed with small decorations. The tape is no longer made, but you can get the same look by stamping satin-style paper or cloth ribbon with mini-stamps. Use pigment ink for your stamping, rather than water-based color, and give your ribbon plenty of time to dry before using it.

GLOW-IN-THE-DARK ICICLES. Also sadly vanished are the glow-in-the-dark icicles and stars that use to hang from trees. You can re-create the look by cutting your own shapes from lightweight cardboard and painting them with glow-in-the-dark craft paint.

ICE CUBE CANDLES. People experimented with all sorts of new crafts in the '50s, from fabric painting to cake decorating to making mosaics. Almost everyone tried candle making at one time or another, and ice cube candles were a favorite. To make one, you need a length of wick a few inches longer than the height of the candle and a small metal disk to weight it to the bottom of the form, a clean cardboard carton such as one half-and-half or orange juice comes in, a pencil, candle wax in your choice of colors, and ice cubes from your freezer. Cut off the top of the carton to make the form the height you want your candle to be. Place the wick in the carton with the weighting disk centered on the bottom of the carton. Position a pencil across the top of the carton and wrap the upper end of the wick around it. Make the wick as straight as possible from top to bottom. Melt the wax in a coffee can placed in a large saucepan half-filled with water. Stir the wax from time to time. Do not let the water and wax come in contact with each other and do not leave the saucepan unattended. When the wax is melted, fill the prepared carton with ice cubes (trying not to disturb your wick) and pour in wax. Do not return the wax to the stove. Discard any unused wax or set it aside for another project. When the wax has hardened enough to hold its shape, remove the pencil, trim the wick, and cut away the carton. Let the candle dry thoroughly before use.

CHRISTMAS GLASSES. Printed glasses were common from the late '40s through the early '60s. Some were kitchen glasses but others were clearly meant for entertaining, patterned with playing card suits or recipes for favorite cocktails. You can make your own '50s-style printed glasses with stamps and StazOn® ink pads, specifically designed to work on glass and other surfaces. Choose stamps that don't exceed the curve of the glass, as rolling the stamp to get full coverage is tricky to say the least. Snowflakes, small snowmen, Santas, and tiny reindeer all make great printed glasses, and the ink pads come in a tempting variety of colors.

SWIZZLE STICKS. Holiday parties of the '50s almost always featured cocktails and highballs rather than beer or wine, and swizzle sticks were standard gear for the well-supplied host. If you're planning a holiday soiree, make your own festive swizzle sticks by wrapping a spiral of tinsel pipe cleaner around the upper inch of a chopstick. Glue the ends to the chopstick, allow to dry completely, and you're ready to go.

Everyone's Gone to the Moon: The 1960s

The '60s started off calmly enough, arriving on the stable shoulders of the 1950s. Still, it didn't take long for chaos to erupt, with a recession, a string of traumatic assassinations, a war that seemed hopeless as well as endless, and a generation of youth determined to do nothing as their parents had. Children who'd spent the '50s wheeling around suburbia on Schwinn bicycles and snacking on Oreos were suddenly trekking to ashrams and eating something called gorp. And when they all came together at Christmas, the result was up for grabs.

In the '60s, what Christmas looked like generally depended on what generation you belonged to. Parents and grandparents stuck with tradition. The youth generation, powerful in numbers as well as spending power, was eager for something new. Or something old—very old. While Mom and Dad were doing the house up in midcentury modern, the kids were embracing looks a century apart. The same daughter sent home from school for wearing a miniskirt one day was just as likely to be sent home for wearing an ankle-length granny dress the next. When it came to Christmas, they had no trouble at all mixing styles. And as for the hippies, who knew what they hung on their trees? Mom and Dad were often afraid to look. Some of the trends that competed in the whiplash decade include:

• **Soft Plastic.** Americans had been buying hard plastic items for almost a generation, so the arrival of soft plastic didn't seem like much of an innovation. In fact, it was. Soft plastic could be molded into **smaller, much more detailed shapes**—pine needles, for example. Because it wasn't brittle, as hard plastic was, there was little breakage during manufacturing and shipping. Best of all, items could be made in parts for later assembly. Soft plastic parts could by dyed to order, making it possible for an artificial poinsettia manufacturer to order stems in green, leaves in red, and yellow stamens for detail—and the ornament market boomed with new decorations.

• **Colors.** The **cool aquas** of the late '50s got even cooler in the early '60s, joined by **white, silver, and platinum**. White had never been a Christmas color before, but paired with icy blues it seemed just the minimalist touch the atomic age desired. Yet you didn't have to look too far to see rebellion brewing. Madras plaid, a trendy fashion fabric of the era, appeared on wrapping paper in the very *un*-Christmasy shades of **orange, purple, yellow, and chartreuse**. **Bright aqua and vivid green** became a popular combination for Christmas; then someone turned up the volume, and by the end of the decade no one was startled to see combinations like **chartreuse, aqua, and hot pink** decking the halls of even the most traditional homes.

• **Frosting.** Frosting began as a hairstyle for blondes who wanted to mimic the sun-streaked, surfer look of the ultracool state of California. Soon everything was frosted—lipstick, fingernail polish, cocktail glasses, and even Christmas decorations. Evergreens suddenly looked naked without a little **flocking**, Christmas balls were often pebbled with grains of **artificial snow**, and wreaths and centerpieces sprouted **silvery leaves**.

• **High Style.** The designed look of the '50s continued into the mid-'60s, but with the **comforting frills edited out** and more **sophisticated touches added**. Napkin rings and centerpieces blossomed on holiday tables. Slices of lemon floated in water glasses. Decorations became decor. The ideal was a kind of **spare elegance**, as personified by Audrey Hepburn on the screen, Jacqueline Kennedy in the White House, and Danish modern furniture in the home. A tree could now be represented by a simple elongated triangle on a card, a trumpeting angel by a flowing scroll of gold across a white field. As for decorations, **a silver bowl with ornament balls, all in the same color**, was more than enough. **Less was more**, the home magazines told readers, and treasured old ornaments, with their hodgepodge of colors and styles, should be left in their boxes. How often the ideal was achieved is open to debate. It was easy enough to choose and send the right cards, but telling the children of the house their favorite spinning, musical, glow-in-the-dark snowman was banished from the scene was another thing altogether.

• **Nature.** A spin-off of the pared-down look was a renewed appreciation for natural materials and nature in general. As early as 1962, one home magazine suggested that readers hang **fresh apples** on the tree in place of ornaments, and fruits and nuts, along with other natural items, became popular materials for centerpieces. Christmas cards frequently depicted **wilderness settings**, usually worked in soft pastels. **Deer** were extremely popular, and a scene of **deer in a snowy forest** was perhaps the most common Christmas card of the decade.

• **The Granny Look.** Inevitably, there was a backlash against the ultramodern trend, and it was led, ironically, by the youth. The same kids who'd brought psychedelia into the house in the first place had a flip side when it came to Christmas. They wanted nothing to do with gaudy soft plastic ornaments, and they weren't too sold on Mom's monochromatic tree, either. They wanted the **cozy, cheerful old-fashioned Christmas** of Granny's day. Not *their* grannies, either, but Granny's granny. And since the youth were driving the culture, **turn-of-the-century touches** began popping up—garlands that looked like strings of **gumdrops**, ornaments that looked like **gingerbread men** or **candy canes**, and **fat twists of yarn** in place of ribbon on packages.

To Make a '60s Tree

Two trends shaped the tree of the '60s. The first was the continued movement away from natural trees. The aluminum tree of the late '50s was still to be seen, but the signature tree of the decade was definitely the **flocked tree**. Since trees had first been brought indoors, people had looked for a way to give them a touch of snow. Pastes of flour and water, dustings of feathers and soap flakes, a DIY kit in the '40s that involved spraying a mixture of chemicals onto the tree with a vacuum cleaner: Nothing to this point was satisfactory. Then, in the '60s, professionally flocked trees became available. They were beautiful, lush, and came in a variety of colors. The most common colors were **white, baby blue, and aqua**, but you could order a tree in any color you wished. **Pink and chartreuse** weren't uncommon, and it's said that Elvis once had a black flocked tree.

The second innovation of the decade was the **themed tree**, introduced by Jacqueline Kennedy during her first Christmas in the White House. The First Lady set the gold standard for simplified elegance, and when her **all-*Nutcracker* tree** was publicized in the press, the idea of decorating a tree around a particular theme was widely copied. Trees adorned in only gold balls and gold and white angels playing golden musical instruments, white trees with white teddy bears in scarlet tunics, trees decorated entirely with candy— all would have been perfectly at home in the '60s.

Even if one didn't want a themed tree, the preferred look for ornaments throughout the '60s can be summed up in one word: limited. A particularly fashionable look for flocked trees was to **dress the tree only with small light and balls in a single color**, and to use balls that were larger than usual. In magazines striving for chic, one seldom saw the gaudy jamboree of ornaments found in ads and Christmas catalogues. The formula for keeping peace in a family split between minimalists and those who preferred the overloaded look was often, as more than one magazine suggested, to put up **multiple trees**, to please each faction.

Get the Look

The '60s spun off enough looks to easily justify the era's key motto: Do your own thing.

Competing looks didn't necessarily play well together, but each had its own charm, and many trends—less clutter, use of natural materials, color schemes instead of a multicolor look—have become today's classics. Here are some ways to add the best of the '60s to your home:

• Renewed appreciation for nature created a particular fad for **driftwood**. Its spare, abstract forms went well with modern homes, and it was easy to decorate for the occasion. You can borrow the look by posing figures of **stylized, modernistic deer** amidst the wood, adding miniature evergreens, or interweaving a spray of pine.

• **Baskets** were another popular item of the '60s, combining the appreciation of natural materials with a desire for a more rustic look. Brighten a corner by crumpling sheets of newspaper to partially fill a large **vine basket**, then piling it with ornament balls.

• Play up a favorite '60s color combination by pairing **blue and green**. Use boughs of **greenery woven with tiny blue lights** to decorate shelves, or adorn a traditional **evergreen wreath with clusters of aqua balls**.

• Christmas **cards with nature scenes** in the ice blues and whites of the era are still popular today. Save the ones that come your way and **put them to good use by cutting them down for place cards or using them to decorate packages** wrapped in pale blue tissue.

• **Della Robbia wreaths and arrangements**, made of **fresh fruits and native plants**, had been extremely popular in Colonial America and enjoyed a revival in the '60s. Recreate the look by arranging evergreen, holly, or ivy down the length of a table or across a mantel, then mixing in nuts in the shell and fruits such as apples, pears, pomegranates, oranges, lemons, limes, and cranberries.

• **Let it snow.** Get a can of **artificial snow** and **add a little frosting** to your decorations. You don't want a heavy coating, just touches of white here and there.

• To echo the **old-fashioned look**, add touches like **glass decanters filled with candy canes**, bowls of wrapped **popcorn balls**, and **mittens** tied to the tree with ribbons.

Crafts

BIRD WREATH

The soft, ethereal look was especially suited to the ice blue pastels of the early 1960s. This lightweight wreath combines that look with a penchant for natural scenes, even if nature was seen through a misty lens and brightened with snowy glitter. These bejeweled little birds in pink, blue, and soft yellow are a perfect match.

MATERIALS:

The inside or outside circle of an 18" embroidery hoop
One roll of 6" wide aqua net, 40 yards long
Tree branch
Small artificial birds
Wire

How to:

Note: If you are buying net off the bolt, you need a total of about 60 square feet of net. Buying by the roll is preferable, as much of the cutting has already been done. I found net by the roll at several sites online, including eBay.

First, find a branch to work with. It should be at least long enough to cross the back of your embroidery hoop, and sturdy enough to attach with wire. Whether or not you want it to have buds and additional branches depends on how many birds you want to add. Make sure your branch is dry and clean. If you want to suggest a wintry look, rub a little white acrylic paint onto it, using your fingers to streak on just a hint of frost. Set the branch aside.

To make the wreath, cut across the 6" wide end of the net on a slight diagonal. Measuring from either point cut at the same diagonal to make a 9½" length. Make a second angled piece that is about 6½" long. These will be your templates, so mark them with a bit of tape

or thread. Because there's a natural tendency to cut larger than the template, using the same template every time will keep your pieces from growing as the project progresses.

Cut several pieces of each length. You don't need to pin the template on, just lay it over the netting to be cut. When you have a stack of four or five pieces, fold in half vertically and cut along the fold to make strips 3" wide. Make equal numbers of both lengths. Don't worry if the ends are a bit jagged or some strips are a bit wider than others—it won't make the slightest bit of difference.

Tie the strips to the embroidery hoop, ends equal and the knot facing you on the narrow edge of the hoop. This will be the front of the wreath. Alternate short strips with long ones. You don't need to tie a double knot; one will hold well. And don't worry too much about scrunching or fluffing or getting the spacing just right—the strips will slide enough for you to adjust later.

Continue cutting and tying until the wreath is full, using the entire roll of net. As you near the end, start fluffing and adjusting. Use the last pieces to fill in any area that needs it, and trim off any tails that stick out too far.

Experiment to find a position for the branch and birds that pleases you. When you find the angle you want, wire the branch to the back side of the wreath.

Attach the birds. The ones shown on page 99 came with convenient alligator clips instead of feet, but if yours don't, just use a bit of wire.

Hang by setting on a hook or make a small loop at the top with a twist of wire.

SEQUINED BALLS

Developed and used during World War II by the military for insulation, Styrofoam was still relatively new to the consumer market in the '60s. One of the first uses it was put to was in the Christmas market, as an alternative to glass ornament balls. It was lightweight, inexpensive, and nearly unbreakable. Best of all, almost anything could be wrapped around it or adhered to its surface. Early Styrofoam balls were often covered with satiny thread. They were fine for what they were, which was an inexpensive version of the real thing. Most people thought of them as fill-ins, bought to make the important ornaments go further. Then someone thought of decorating them in a way traditional balls couldn't compete with, and the embellished, beaded, and bejeweled balls became a hit.

MATERIALS NEEDED FOR EACH BALL:

$3^1/_2"$ Styrofoam ball

2 yards of 6-mm string sequins

Approximately 4 feet of ¼" wide Terrifically Tacky Tape

Ornament cap with pronged loop

Straight pins, small sharp scissors

How to:

The preparation for this craft may seem a bit lengthy, but don't despair—once everything is in place, the actual wrapping goes very quickly.

To begin, wind tacky tape once around the ball in a belt that divides the ball in half. Press the tape firmly so that it adheres to the ball. Don't remove the liner, but peel it back a bit so the end of the tape can cover the starting point and you have two tabs of liner. Now made a second belt that begins and ends where the first one did, and divides the ball into four even quarters. Make two more belts so that you end up with a ball that's divided into eight sections, like an orange. The bands should crisscross each other at the "north pole" (where you began) and at the "south pole," directly opposite it. At the north pole you should have eight tabs of liner that have been peeled back from the tape.

Set the ball aside and take up the string of sequins. Use a pin to unlace the threads and slide off three or four sequins. Don't cut the thread or let it get tangled—the purpose of this is to give you long enough ends of thread to knot. When you have enough thread to tie, make a double knot and trim the thread ends.

Pull back an inch or so of liner on all eight liner ends to expose the tape. Use straight pins to pin the liners to the ball to hold them out of your way as you work.

Press the end of the sequin string to the center of the north pole, pressing it firmly to the crisscrossed tape. Now begin wrapping the ball in a spiral, making sure the top of the row you are laying down overlaps the bottom of the row above. You will see as you go that the sequins have a natural tendency to curve around the ball and overlap. If you do go a bit off course, lift the sequin string and reposition it. Continue peeling back liner and wrapping sequin string, pressing sequins down firmly as you go.

When you get to the bottom, trim as much of the liner off as possible. After the last sequin is in place, cut the sequin string, leaving about an inch of extra sequins. As you did at the top, gently unthread the sequins to give yourself enough thread to knot. Tie and trim off the extra thread. This is now the top of your ornament, and the place where you began is the bottom.

Take up an ornament loop fitted with a cap. Work the prongs of the loop between the sequins. Push them down into the Styrofoam ball until the cap rests on top of the ball. Your ornament is finished and ready to hang.

SNOWFLAKE WRAPPING PAPER

People were pickier about gift wrap in the '60s than they had been in the past. If it was going under the tree, it had to complement the decor. And if it was going out of town, it had to reflect the up-to-date and finely tuned tastes of the sender. Failing to find the right paper at the store was no excuse and, since it was the age of spare elegance, one could always fall back on pure white with a few well-placed embellishments.

MATERIALS:

Inexpensive wrapping paper with a plain white back
  (The front doesn't matter.)
Assorted snowflake mini-stamps
Ink pad for stamping
Stickles Glitter Glue in same color as ink pad

How to:

Cut a piece of wrapping paper to fit the package you want to wrap. Place facedown on a thick magazine. The blank white side should be facing you. Stamp random snowflakes over the entire surface, moving the paper as necessary so that you are always stamping on the magazine.

Place a dot of glitter glue at the center of each snowflake. Add random dots of glitter glue across the open areas of the paper. Allow to dry overnight.

ICE BRANCHES

In the '60s, people brought all sorts of wild plants into their homes to decorate with—cattails, milkweed pods, branches and berries and grasses. Sometimes the flora was used as is, but often it got a boost of gold spray paint, a dusting of artificial snow, or some other embellishment. Of course, it didn't take long for some manufacturer to figure out how to make branches appear to have come straight from the Siberian sets of *Doctor Zhivago*, and sold them for a nice profit by the branch. These are so inexpensive and easy to make you can have as many as you like.

MATERIALS:

Branches

Acrylic paint (if you want colored branches)

Mod Podge Original Gloss

Colorfill Diamond Vase Filler plastic ice crystals

1" wide acrylic-style brush, newspaper to cover floor

How to:

First, decide where you want to work. This isn't a difficult craft, but it is a messy one. I strongly recommend doing it on a bare floor that can be easily swept, as no matter how much paper you put down, the plastic ice crystals have a tendency to end up all over the place.

Lay sheets of newspaper in a large enough area for your branches to rest on.

Many ice branches of the era were painted white, but of course you can paint them any shade you want. These were left bare for a more natural look.

Whether you paint them or not, make sure your branches are completely dry when you begin.

Quickly paint your first branch with the Mod Podge, front and bank. If you have a very large branch, do only a section at a time. Use plenty of glue. When you have finished painting both sides, turn the first side back up and gently pour vase filler wherever the branch has been painted with glue. Most of it won't stick, but that's okay—you're not trying for solid coverage, just clinging ice crystals. When you've done the first side, turn the branch over gently and do the other side. Go back over both sides, adding more crystals where you see bare spots. If necessary, dab on more glue where needed. Be patient. You'll find that as the glue begins to set, fewer crystals will fall off.

Prop the finished branches up so the parts with glue and crystals aren't directly on the paper but the branch is still horizontal. Let dry overnight.

MARABOU TREAT CUP

By the end of the '60s, the influence of pop art and pop culture could be seen everywhere. Traditional forms and objects were recast with a fun, funky edge, like the Beatles quasi-military, Popsicle-colored coats on the cover of the *Sgt. Pepper's Lonely Hearts Club Band* album, or work boots in gold lamé. Even Christmas didn't escape, especially where cosmic color combinations were concerned. Pay homage to the era with a classic treat cup done in mod colors.

MATERIALS:

2 sheets 8½" x 11" card stock, any color, for interior sleeve

2 sheets scrapbook paper, for exterior

1 foot marabou trim

¾ yard ribbon, ⅝" wide

Paper punch

Double-sided adhesive tape

Regular adhesive tape, scissors

How to:

To make the liner, draw and cut out four isosceles triangles, 9" tall with a 3" base from the card stock. (See illustration page 110.) Lay two pieces right side down with the long edges meeting but not overlapping. Tape together with a single long piece of ordinary adhesive tape. Trim off any excess tape. Join the third piece to the first two in the same way, then the fourth piece.

You should now be able to fold the pieces, taped side out, into a cone-shaped sleeve. All you have to do is join the edges of the two end pieces. To do this, edge one of the pieces with a length of tape, positioning it so that the bottom edge adheres to the piece and the top edge is free. Line up the triangles so their edges meet and press the free edge of the tape down onto the edge of triangle. Set the finished sleeve aside.

From decorative, scrapbook-weight paper, cut four trapezoids that are 9" tall, 4" at the base, and 1" at the top. (See illustration below.) Lay one piece facedown and fold ½" in along the two sides (shown by dotted line on illustration). Do this to both sides of all four pieces.

Now join the pieces together by placing a length of double-sided tape on the right side of the folded strip and joining it to the right side of the other folded strip, so that the two pieces of the cone line up. Join the other two pieces to the first two in the same way. You should now be able to fold the pieces, right side out and taped flaps in, into a cone-shaped sleeve. Trim the taped flaps at an angle at the narrow end, so they don't interfere with the point. Press each flap so it lays flat and to the side. All you have to do is join the edges of the two end pieces, as you did before. Lay the cone on one side and use the pencil to press down the flap.

Slide the interior sleeve into the outer cone.

To attach the ribbon, make a hole on two facing sides with your paper punch, about 3/8" down from the opening and centered. Thread each end of the ribbon through from the inside to the outside. Adjust the length and tie a knot to keep the ribbon from sliding.

Wrap marabou trim around the top. Fasten the trim in place with bits of double-sided tape.

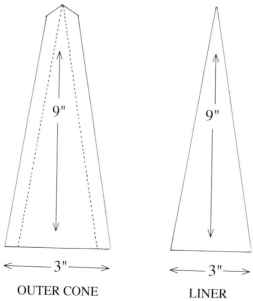

OUTER CONE   LINER

Quick Crafts

SNOWFLAKE STENCIL NAPKINS. Give plain cloth napkins a custom look with a snowflake punch, peel-and-stick-paper, a tube of acrylic paint, and a stipple brush or wedge sponge. Punch the snowflake shape out of the peel-and-stick paper. You're not going to use the shape itself, so set that aside for another project. Peel the liner off the paper and adhere it to the napkin, pressing the edges down firmly. Use a brush or sponge to pounce paint onto the stencil. When the paint is dry, peel away the stencil.

TWIST-AND-TIE NAPKIN RINGS. You can make quick napkin rings from inexpensive snowflake charms and tinsel pipe cleaners or ribbon. Cut the pipe cleaners or ribbon in lengths, attach a snowflake to each end, and wrap around the napkin. Twist pipe cleaner ends together to hold in place or tie the ribbon in a bow.

POMANDER BALLS. Add spice to the Della Robbia look by sticking whole cloves into oranges, lemons, or other citrus fruits. Dot them on at random or use the cloves to create patterns, such as vertical sections or a spiral that winds around the fruit from top to bottom. Mix the pomanders with other pieces of whole fresh fruit, pile several in a footed bowl, or attach a loop of ribbon to them and hang from the tree.

SPUTNIKS. This is a great way to use up all those little lengths of tinsel pipe cleaners left over from other crafts. Spray a Styrofoam ball with silver spray paint or paint with glue and sprinkle with glitter. Then stick all those odd lengths and colors of tinsel pipe cleaners into the ball.

GRANNY BALLS. These homespun balls are quite pretty piled together in a basket. To make them you'll need narrow strips of fabric and Styrofoam balls. Prairie flower prints were very popular in the '60s, so look through your scrap bag for bits with a floral motif. To make, tear the fabric into narrow strips and wind onto the balls as you'd wind yarn. Fasten the ends with straight pins pushed into the ball.

Craft a Little Sweetness: Easy Homemade Candy

Treats of the season have always been a wonderful part of the decorating excitement, and many items we take for granted today—such as fresh oranges—were treasured luxuries in the past. Other foods that would have been set out include nuts in the shell (nutcrackers with matching picks being as common in most homes then as cocktail glasses are today), candy canes or peppermints, and popped corn, which was often mixed with raisins or accompanied by crisp red apples. Major candy—such as chocolates, gumdrops, or the colorful satin pillows and pieces of ribbon hard candy we think of as traditional—were held in reserve for stockings or handed out as special treats.

Happily, traditional Christmas candy is still being made, and you can find a seller online if none is to be had in your local stores. In the meantime, dress up your candy dishes with these easy homemade sweets.

Mackinac Island Fudge

Mackinac Island, the Michigan resort island famous for its horse-drawn carriages and lack of cars, has been drawing vacationers for well over one hundred years. No fudge lover who's tasted classic Mackinac Island fudge will ever forget its distinct, caramel–brown sugary undertones. Quicker and easier to make than most vintage fudge recipes, this candy needs no expensive chocolate and no candy thermometer—it dates back to the days when people cooked by the clock, and all good things came from unsweetened cocoa powder.

INGREDIENTS:

½ cup whole milk

½ cup butter (don't substitute)

½ cup light brown sugar

½ cup white sugar

⅛ teaspoon salt

1 teaspoon vanilla extract

2 cups powdered sugar

½ cup unsweetened cocoa powder

Directions:

Combine the milk, butter, brown sugar, white sugar, and salt in a heavy saucepan. Cook over medium heat, stirring frequently. Bring mixture to a boil and boil for six minutes, stirring constantly.

Remove from heat and stir in the vanilla, powdered sugar, and cocoa powder. Beat until smooth and thick.

You can put this fudge in a pan, but why not do as they do on Mackinac? Roll it into a log and wrap in two layers of plastic wrap. Whichever way you choose, chill for about twenty minutes before cutting. Slice rounds from the log and cut in semicircles to serve.

Caramels

Caramels go back hundreds of years and, along with chocolate, are one of the key tastes and textures people seek in candy. This recipe, at least fifty years old but probably older, produces a wonderfully soft and creamy caramel and can easily be doubled for giving as gifts. You will need to use a candy thermometer, but other than that the recipe's a snap. For a modern twist, sprinkle some sea salt over the top before cutting.

INGREDIENTS:

½ cup white sugar

½ cup packed light brown sugar

½ cup light corn syrup

½ cup evaporated milk (not sweetened condensed)

1 cup heavy cream

½ cup unsalted butter

1¼ teaspoons vanilla extract

Directions:

Line a 9" x 9" pan with parchment. Let the ends of the parchment extend over the sides.

In a heavy saucepan, combine all the ingredients except the vanilla.

Gradually bring to a boil, starting over a low flame and increasing to medium and medium high as the mixture melds together.

Stir continually, scraping the sides and bottom of the saucepan often to keep crystals from forming. Monitor the heat with a candy thermometer, making sure the tip of the thermometer is not touching the bottom of the pan.

When the mixture is heated to 250°F, remove from heat and stir in the vanilla.

Pour into a pan and let cool completely, until set.

Lift the caramel block out of the pan and place on a cutting board. Cut into bite-size squares and wrap in individual squares of waxed paper. For an added festive touch, cut squares of red and green cellophane and wrap these as a cover over the waxed paper.

Turtles

Turtles first appeared during the Depression, the creation of confectioners Bobbi and Gordon Hooper, who had learned their craft from Mary See of See's Candies fame. The Hoopers set up production in Oakland, California, and candy orders were dashingly delivered on a Harley-Davidson motorcycle. Turtles quickly became popular throughout the Bay Area, and other confectioners began producing their own versions. The originals were coated with milk chocolate, but try mixing milk and semisweet together, swirling melted white chocolate into dark, or coating completely with white chocolate.

INGREDIENTS:

Toasted, salted whole pecan halves
Caramels made from the recipe on page 115
Block-style milk chocolate for melting

Directions:

On a sheet of waxed paper or baker's parchment, arrange four pecans in an X. Flatten a caramel over the center to hold them together. You now have the body with the protruding paws of your turtle. Repeat for as many turtles as you wish to make.

In a heavy saucepan or double boiler, heat the chocolate over a low flame or simmering water until it is completely melted and smooth, stirring often.

Using a spatula edge to guide the stream, drizzle the melted chocolate over each turtle to completely cover. Cool, allowing to set completely. If your turtles cool but still don't seem to be firm enough, pop them into the fridge. When firm, trim away the excess chocolate and store in a tin or covered plastic container at room temperature.

Don't throw away the excess chocolate. Remelt it with whatever's left over from making the turtles and drop in small round puddles onto a fresh sheet of waxed paper. Before the chocolate sets, liberally sprinkle with tiny dragées, edible glitter, or sprinkles to make nonpareil wafers.

Peanut Butter Cornflake Clusters

Need candy in the next half hour? Here's a remarkably speedy recipe with the added virtue of being delicious. The recipe also works well with a variety of add-ins, including chocolate chips and white chocolate chips, peanuts, pecans, raisins, and coconut. Just add an extra spoonful of peanut butter to compensate for the extra dryness.

INGREDIENTS:

½ cup white sugar

½ cup light corn syrup

1 cup peanut butter (I use crunchy.)

2 cups cornflakes

Directions:

Mix the sugar and corn syrup in a saucepan over medium heat. Increase the heat and bring to a boil, then immediately lower the heat and add the peanut butter.

Stir until the peanut butter is melted and thoroughly combined.

Remove from heat. Add the cornflakes and stir to coat well.

Drop by spoonfuls onto waxed paper. Allow to cool, and then store in a tin or plastic container.

This will make about thirty clusters, give or take, depending on how big you make them.

Butterscotch Haystacks

This recipe, like Peanut Butter Cornflake Clusters, dates back to the '60s, an era when people apparently discovered that if you combine almost anything crunchy with almost anything sweet and melty, you will almost certainly end up with something delicious. There were numerous such recipes floating around, two of the most famous involving melted chocolate chips with cornflakes and melted chocolate chips with Rice Krispies. Not to mention the recipe that got the ball rolling way back in the '30s, Rice Krispies Treats. While some still scoff at such homey little treats, anyone who does is probably bitterly clinging to his chocolate-dipped gourmet potato chips.

INGREDIENTS:

12-ounce bag of butterscotch morsels

5-ounce can of chow mein noodles

    (not ramen-style, but the old-fashioned, fully cooked, crunchy style)

Directions:

In a heavy saucepan, melt the butterscotch morsels over low heat, stirring continuously. When the morsels are completely melted, stir in the entire can of chow mein noodles and remove from heat.

Drop by teaspoons in mounds onto waxed paper. Let these cool completely, and then store in a tin or plastic container.

Almond Bark

I believe the secret of good almond bark is using a mix of chocolates, just as the secret of making good pizza is using more than one kind of cheese. My personal preference is to combine milk chocolate and a strong semisweet chocolate in a 2 to 1 ratio. Your preference may be different, so be prepared to undertake the arduous and demanding task of making this often to find the right combination.

Note: You'll notice I don't temper the chocolate. This means that, with time, the bark may develop the slight dusty look and crumbly texture characteristic of untempered chocolate. By that time, however, this delicious stuff will have long since been eaten, which is why I don't bother.

INGREDIENTS:

12 ounces good, block-style milk chocolate for melting

6 ounces of good, block-style semisweet chocolate for melting

8 ounces roasted, salted whole almonds

Directions:

Line a baking sheet with baker's parchment or waxed paper.

Chop the chocolates roughly and place in heavy saucepan or double boiler. Make sure the pot is big enough to accommodate the almonds as well.

Melt the chocolate over very low heat, stirring frequently and watching to make sure chocolate doesn't begin to clump or seize.

When the chocolate is smooth and melted, stir in the almonds. Immediately turn out onto the lined baking sheet and spread in a thin, even layer.

Allow to cool to room temperature, then move to the refrigerator to set completely. Break into pieces and store in a tin or plastic container at room temperature.

Buttercrunch

Buttercrunch (often referred to as toffee) must be one of the earliest candies in the world, a simple combination of butter and sugar fused into a deliciously splintery sheet. People are fond of dressing it up with the addition of nuts and coatings of chocolate, and you're free to do so if you wish, but I feel that golden mouthful of pure, unadulterated buttercrunch is too delicious to improve upon. You will need a candy thermometer for this recipe.

INGREDIENTS:

1/2 cup unsalted butter, cut into several pieces

1/8 teaspoon coarse salt

1 cup white sugar

1/4 cup light brown sugar, firmly packed

1 teaspoon vanilla extract

Directions:

Line a baking sheet with baker's parchment or waxed paper.

Place 2 tablespoons of water in a heavy saucepan and add all the ingredients except the vanilla. Cook over a low flame until the butter and sugars have melted completely.

Clip the candy thermometer to the pan, making sure the tip is immersed but not touching the pan itself.

Increase the flame to medium high and continue to cook, stirring and scraping the pan once a minute to prevent any crystallizing and guard against scorching.

Monitoring the heat continually, bring the mixture to 300°F. When you reach that temperature, stir in vanilla and immediately remove from heat.

Pour the mixture quickly over prepared baking sheet. Try to pour as even a sheet as possible. If there are places that are too thick, spread gently with a spatula. Hot buttercrunch doesn't respond well to handling, so fuss with it as little as possible.

Let set overnight to cool and cure. Do not cover, which can make your candy tacky.

The next day, break into pieces and store in a covered tin.

Art Portfolio

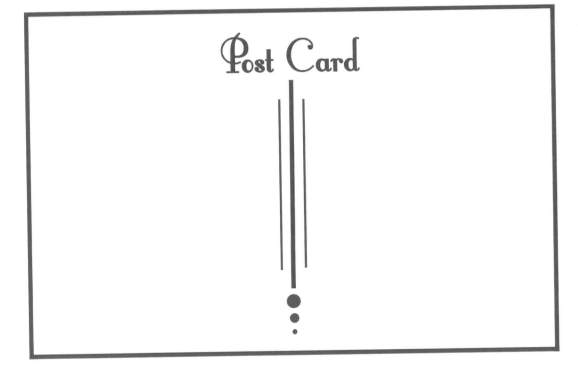

FROM OUR HOUSE
TO YOUR HOUSE

Happy

Holidays

Post Card

SANTA

by the

WASHERS

129

130

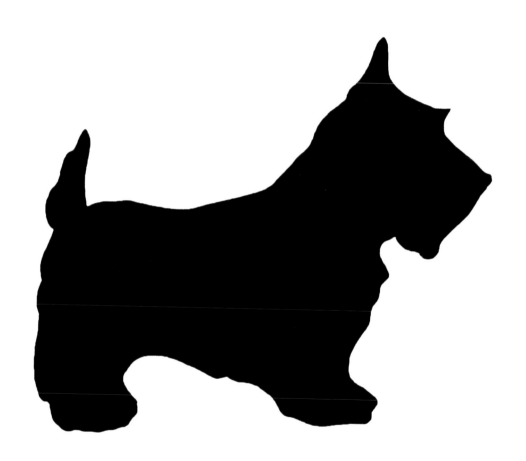

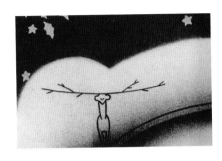

131

Christmas Greetings

CHRISTMAS CHEER

132

BEST WISHES

Season's Greetings

To: From:

To

From

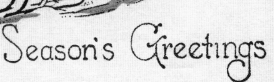

Season's Greetings

For

christmas cheer

DO NOT
UNTIL

UNTIE
DEC. 25

MERRY
CHRISTMAS

DO NOT OPEN

UNTIL
DEC. 25TH

GREETINGS

136

Greetings

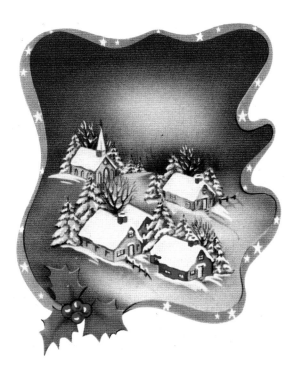

Merry Christmas

Christmas is a jolly time,
 Any way you take it,
But what a dear and happy time
 Friends like you do make it!

SING A SONG OF CHRISTMAS

RUST CRAFT, U.S.A.   46

MERRY
CHRISTMAS,
May the Yuletide's
radiant light
Make your whole world
glad and bright!

143

SOURCES FOR MATERIALS

GENERAL SUPPLIES

eBay, Jo-Ann Fabrics, and Michaels: General supplies such as glue, glitter, glitter glue, tape, etc.

SPECIFIC SUPPLIES

Acme Notions (acmenotions.com): Red border stripe dish towels.

BJ Craft Supplies (bjcraftsupplies.com): Bump chenille, tinsel pipe cleaners.

Blümchen (blumchen.com): Crepe paper, lametta.

Buz-Line (buz-line.com): Scotch Positionable Mounting Adhesive.

Creative Gift Packaging (creativegiftpackaging.com): Cellophane by the roll.

Dollar Bead (dollarbead.com): Glass beads.

eBay (ebay.com): Vintage cards, string sequins, Ping-Pong balls, nylon net.

Etsy (etsy.com): Santa jingle bell charms.

Factory Direct Craft (factorydirectcraft.com): Antique-looking artificial candles, unfinished wooden beads, artificial birds, small silver bells, 20-mm silver glittered ornament balls, Styrofoam balls.

Kate's Paperie (katespaperie.com): Wired gold mesh ribbon, marabou.

Paper Addict (paperaddict.com): Vintage-looking Christmas paper.

Save-on-Crafts (save-on-crafts.com): Clear glass ornament balls, vase filler.

Silver Crow Creations (silvercrowcreations): Small bottle-brush trees.